DATE DUE

The C. G. JUNG Haunted Prophet

by Paul J. Stern

A DELTA BOOK

A DELTA BOOK

Published by Dell Publishing Co., Inc.
1 Dag Hammarskjold Plaza
New York, New York 10017

Manufactured in the United States of America

Reprinted by arrangement with George Braziller, Inc.

Delta ® TM 755118, Dell Publishing Co., Inc.

ISBN: 0-440-54744-X

First Delta printing—April 1977

CONTENTS

Contents

PREFACE

From early adolescence, Carl Jung was haunted by a sense of prophetic mission. The prophet, in his eyes, was chosen through the agency of "fate" to proclaim a new truth or reestablish an ancient, forgotten one. His own prophetic revelation was that of the Reality of the Soul.

On the face of it, Jung's prophetic message had the earmarks of an anachronism. By 1900, the notion of soul had been pretty much excised from the minds and vocabularies of most Western intellectuals. To promulgate, in the solemn tone peculiar to Jung, "the timeless and spaceless reality of the human soul" must have struck most of his colleagues as rather quixotic, if they paid any heed to the message at all. Nor were the Protestant (and Catholic) theologians, who were Jung's real intended audience, more likely to hail an opaque doctrine that amounted to a deification of the Self. To complain, as Jung ceaselessly did, that his message was not appreciated or fell upon deaf ears was to evince a remarkable social blindness.

It was Carl Jung's misfortune to have lived at a historic juncture that was not quite ready for his gospel of inwardness. He so wanted to be a seer honored in his own time, but he had to disguise himself as a scientist. Born too early for his own joy —and knowing it—he had to console himself with the thought of posthumous vindication. But much as he yearned for recognition, he did not want to buy it at the price of martyrdom. Hence he arranged for the most revealing of his works, his memoirs, to be published after his death.

In his book on Luther, Erik Erikson outlined some characteristics of the "great man" who reshapes social and cultural reality: "Deeply and pathologically upset, but possessed both by the vision of a new (or renewed) world order and by the need (and the gift) to transform masses of men, such a man makes his individual 'patienthood' representative of a universal one, and promises 'to solve for all what he could not solve for himself alone.' "[1]

While Carl Jung was beyond question endowed with the requisite depth of pathology, it may have been the wrong kind for his time and place. Also his visionary powers, as well as his talents as demagogue, were circumscribed and lacked crispness. Hence, he has been confined so far to the limbo of cult heroes who have filed for more exalted status. History is still examining his claim, and may yet certify him as culture hero. Jung, at any rate, counted on a favorable verdict. He saw himself as herald of the dawning Age of Aquarius—an age of mutants bound to usher in radical changes in human modes of feeling

[1] My friend Charles McArthur has called this the theory of the hero as a flake.

and thought. He may not have been completely off the mark. The era of space flight and new planetary mythologies is indeed likely to spawn, and to move to center stage, new modal personalities more attuned to Jung's invisible realities than were his contemporaries.

But if Jung's ultimate status as prophet is still in doubt, his interest as a *case*, as an exemplary figure, is not. His life-story is a compelling parable that illustrates the creative uses of incipient madness. It is a tale of battles waged, and at least partly won, by an intrinsically vulnerable personality against the inchoate psychic forces that lurk beneath consciousness in everybody, and that in Jung's case, for reasons partly traceable to his somber childhood, were particularly virulent.

In his relentless war against what he called his inner demons, Jung devised methods of exorcism that had relevance beyond his personal struggle. During his youth, he had dreamed of becoming a military engineer and building impregnable fortresses, but he realized in early manhood that he could not contain the enemy within by erecting higher and higher psychic walls. The decisive turn came when Jung, seeing the hopelessness of clenched resistance, decided to let go, to affirm and embrace the haunting psychotic "unrealities" whose destructive power he dreaded, not without reason.

Comparing James Joyce with Joyce's schizophrenic daughter whom he had treated, Jung once remarked that the creative artist plunges of his own volition into the scary psychic depths into which the drowning psychotic is pulled against his will. While Jung's own descent into the psychic netherworld was less self-propelled than he liked to think, he was bold and wily enough to ultimately consent to the inevitable and thus gain a foothold in a new, larger reality.

C. G. Jung—The Haunted Prophet

Jung had money and he was socially protected enough to be able, during the crucial period 1913 to 1917, to devote much of his energy to confronting the hallucinatory voices and visions assailing him. By giving these psychotic apparitions their due, by paying close attention to their often cryptic messages, and by finding their core of reality, he was able to appropriate and thus to disarm them. Such a synthesis is, of course, preferable to the pauper's compromises available to those squeezed by circumstances and the narrow horizons of their caretakers— compromises that force them to consign most, if not all, of their psychotic reality to the slagheap of the merely "imaginary" in order for them to be readmitted to the world of the sane.

Jung's solution was that he simultaneously personalized and mythologized the psychotic forces within him. Driven by his own extremity, he speculated about archetypes and the collective unconscious as part of an attempt at self-healing. The genesis of these concepts, of course, does not prejudge their validity or lack of it.

But if Jung's taming of his unruly demons is a magnificent example of an inner battle won against great odds, it also exemplifies the limitations, and the costs to the personality, of this sort of triumph. There are no total victories to be gained on psychic battlefields. The early contours of Jung's personality defined the limits of its growth. Even after his heroic self-analysis, Jung was not free of major blind spots; to the attentive if not unsympathetic reader of his work their presence is obvious. His emphatic spirituality blinded him to the darker specifics of much that went on inside him, but it also mitigated the rude shocks administered to him by an omnipotent, and in his case peculiarly anguishing, universe. And while it is true that his private mythology, which he strove to transform into a universal one, revealed to him hidden facets of reality, it also mercifully concealed aspects of it that he would have found unbearable. The haze of abstraction and abstractedness shimmering around his utterances is symptomatic of his evasions.

Yet it would be ungracious to demand from Carl Jung a degree of openness unavailable to him. A German poet has said that no one ever reaches such insight into truth as would cancel the preconditions of his own existence. The foundations of Jung's existence were shaky. Yet he managed to erect on them a life structure that, while not devoid of deep flaws and marks of contrivance, attained the harsh grandeur of a work of art wrought from intractable material.

C.G. JUNG—The Haunted Prophet

1

THE MYTH OF
CARL JUNG

Carl Jung viewed the story of his life as the unfolding of a myth. When, already in his eighties, he quashed earlier misgivings and started to write his autobiography,[1] with the help of his secretary Aniela Jaffé, it was this personal myth much more than the factual events of his life that he set out to capture. Shunning the notion of reflecting the "objective" truth about himself—a goal he thought impossible in any case—he wanted to make sure that he was telling *his* truth, which he equated with his *fable.* Thus to set down his "autobiography," which he used to refer to in ironic quotation marks, was for him a poetic venture, a serried and imaginative recasting of his lived

[1] *Memories, Dreams, Reflections,* hereafter referred to as "Memories."

and remembered reality. Poetry, like every art form, defines its essence by leaving out what it views as nonessential. Carl Jung's "Memories," as has often been noted, tell us very little about the external events of his life and next to nothing—with the notable exceptions of his parents and Sigmund Freud—about the people who accompanied or crossed his life's path. But through this process of excision, the memories manage to project an image of intense inwardness that, in Jung's case, is more telling than the most minute chronicle of his actions and interactions could ever be.[2]

Thus Jung's mythologizing of his past, in his autobiography, was not naive or unintentional. The telling of the myth became itself part of the myth, a "matter of fate," in Jung's words, an ineluctable task "imposed from within." An inveterate mythmaker, Jung saw the fine hand of fate everywhere, even if its tools were such unlikely figures as the shrewd German-American publisher Kurt Wolff whose urgings finally overcame Jung's often-stated reluctance to work on a self-portrayal. In fact, only a short time before he discovered its fatedness, Jung had written that any attempt on his part to record his life-story would be fatuous: "If one is sincere, or believes one is, it is a delusion or a sign of bad taste."

In telling his fable Jung, like any mythographer, was not above rearranging and embellishing his past, not above lapsing now and then into a bit of mystification, of himself and others. "Memories" is a multifaceted work, self-apology as much as logbook of an inner journey, self-glorification in the same breath as self-defense, a canny propaganda tract promoting the

---

[2]It would be erroneous to attribute the extreme solipsism of Jung's "Memories" to old age. For Carl Jung, old age was a culmination, not a shipwreck; it accentuated, rather than corroded, the outlines of his personality.

image of the "wise old man" that Jung wanted to bequeath to posterity. Jung's "Memories" is, in a sense, a self-conscious gospel and Bible of the Jungian dispensation, in the form of a parable. Since Jung, not without reason, had little faith in the intellectual and literary gifts of his more devout apostles, he decided to lend a helping hand in preparing his own transfiguration.

Carl Jung would have viewed almost anything that could have befallen him as fateful and portentous. In fact, one of the most striking features of his autobiography is how he inflates experiences that most other people would consider trivial to the dimensions of portents. As it happened, life cooperated and presented him with much experiential and biographical raw material that lent itself readily to mythical elaboration. Jung found in his family tradition, ready-made, a story of legendary origins to satisfy the most exalted aspirations in this line. And toward the end of his life, he found himself in the unusual position of being able to describe to others his own resurrection from death, or a close facsimile thereof. Before launching upon our story proper, let us briefly look at these two exemplary Jungian myths.

In 1944, when he was sixty-eight years old, Carl Jung had a severe heart attack. Near death, drugged and delirious, he had a glorious vision. He was floating high in stellar space, looking down on the bluish silvery globe of the earth far below him.[3] Leaving the earth farther and farther behind, he suddenly saw, a short distance away in space, a big solitary rock containing

[3] Jung's view from his lofty height, which he described in considerable detail, strikingly resembled the wide-angle photos of the globe taken by astronauts two decades later. But in 1944 such sights were still beyond the range of ordinary human experience.

a temple whose entrance was illuminated by a thousand small flames of coconut oil. Jung knew that he was to enter this temple, that to pass its threshold meant dying, and that death was going to answer all his questions. Jung yearned with all his being for this ultimate consummation. But at this very moment a messenger from the earth, in the guise of Jung's doctor, arrived and said that Jung was not allowed yet to depart, that he was still needed below. With this unwelcome news, the whole vision collapsed. Glum and dispirited, Jung returned to the dull, astringent world of the living. Feeling exiled, he listlessly watched the slow mending of his body. The thought of food nauseated him, the presence of people grated on his nerves. He bore a grudge toward the doctor who had meddled with his dying.

The letters Jung wrote after his recovery had a decidedly posthumous ring. "What happens after death is so unspeakably glorious," he wrote to one correspondent, "that our imagination and our feelings do not suffice to form even an approximate conception of it." A bit later, he wrote to his American student Kristine Mann, then dying of cancer, that in dying the only difficult part was "to get rid of the body, to get quite naked and void of the world and the ego-will." One had only to renounce one's crazed will to live, in order to experience the beginning of one's "truly *real* life" with "everything you were meant to be and never reached. It is something ineffably grand." However disappointed Jung may have been about having to resume his hard life on earth, the events surrounding his return from the gates of death sustained and nourished his sense of fateful election.

As to Carl Jung's myth of origins, it was related to his grandfather Carl Gustav Jung (1794–1864), rumored to have been an illegitimate son of the great Goethe. The grandson was so much taken with the legend of this illustrious illegitimacy that in his head it became a quasi-certainty. Goethe was, to him, the highest embodiment of creativity, his Faust, the modern counterpart to Oedipus. In letters and talks with friends, Jung often alluded to *the* great-grandfather as if his blood tie to Goethe were a proven fact. And if, on occasion, he felt called upon to repudiate the legend of his descent as "annoying," he usually did so in a tone that denied his denial.

The elder Jung himself seems to have attached less weight to this question. In his diaries, he mentioned only in passing that during a visit to Weimar he had caught a glimpse of Goethe, at some distance, and from behind. This view of his alleged begetter's backside was apparently his only contact with him. The threads linking his mother, the volatile Sophie Ziegler, with the great poet seem equally slender. The whole story was apparently based on some far-fetched surmises and on Goethe's public image as a great and prodigal amorist; but this image was itself a myth, invented and propagated by unworldly German professors of literature who mistook Goethe's poems as factual documents.

Whether a son of Goethe or not, the elder C. G. Jung was an imposing and somewhat legendary figure in his own right. A German emigrant, whose liberalism had gotten him into trouble with the reactionary Prussian authorities, he had come in 1822 to the University of Basel as a poor young lecturer in medicine. Within one year, he was promoted to full professor, and later served as rector of the university as well as Grand Master of the Swiss Lodge of Freemasons. Much admired and gossiped about by his fellow-citizens, he passed for eccentric, but his easy charm took the edge off his more disconcerting oddities. Typical of him was the story of how he acquired his second wife. After the death of his first wife, a Frenchwoman, Jung wooed Sophie Frey, daughter of Basel's mayor and eighteen years his junior. He was rebuffed, whereupon he headed straight for his favorite pub and asked the waitress Elisabeth Reyenthaler to marry him. To the consternation of the status-conscious Baselites, the left-handed marriage between the professor and the waitress actually took place. When Elisabeth died three years later, the twice-widowed Jung asked again for the hand of Sophie Frey and this time was accepted. Mayor Frey's financial fortunes had deteriorated by then, and this may have made the fortyish professor more palatable as son-in-law.

Both in terms of his personal life and in terms of his fabled descent, he left the grandson named after him the lineaments of a precious myth. In particular, the belief in his kinship with Goethe—however tenuous its basis—was vital to Carl Jung. He believed in its truth because he needed to. (And in his eyes, an intense belief was self-validating.) For he was born into a bleak and harsh world, made endurable only by its transfiguration through myth.

2

A WORLD
HE NEVER MADE

Carl Jung's early years in the parsonage of Klein-Hüningen, near Basel, were darkened by the shadow of parental strife. Of delicate health, he suffered from infancy with eczemas, fevers, croup, and choking fits—ailments which, as an old man looking back, he was to connect with intimations of domestic sorrows.

Carl's ill-matched and ill-starred parents, the Reverend Paul Jung and Emilie Jung-Preiswerk, a minister's daughter, were trapped in a marriage gone sour, with no way out. The birth of Carl, welcomed at first, soon sharpened their sense of entrapment. By the time Carl was three, Emilie, the more vital of the parents, left the family for several months. A chronic ailment, mysterious and hard to diagnose, made it advisable— or, at least, excusable—for her to spend some time at a hospital in the city. But the Basel polyclinic was no Magic Mountain, and after a few months she had to return to the parsonage whose atmosphere her son was later to describe as "unbreathable."

On the face of things, it was largely the morose humor of the Reverend Dr. Jung that poisoned the domestic atmosphere. Paul Jung was a man disappointed by life. Amiable, bland, and somewhat of a blunderer, he had hoped in his youth to become a professor of Oriental languages. His university years had been his Golden Age, the era when he dreamed his modest dreams of glory. But, having finished his doctoral thesis on an Arabic version of the Song of Songs, he had to settle for the post of a country parson. When his marriage turned out not to be what he had imagined, when he found himself eclipsed by his energetic wife and ignored or pitied by his willful, secretive son, when he lost his small capital, and, in addition to his other misfortunes, was beset by constant health worries, he began to think of himself as a failure and sank into a gloomy apathy.

His son Carl, who for reasons of his own tended to play down the importance of external hardship, decided very early on that Paul Jung's miserable decline was the direct result of a *spiritual* crisis. Carl had somehow managed to convince himself that his father, the professional man of God, was being destroyed by unacknowledged religious doubts. As Carl saw it, his spiritually wounded father had neither simple faith nor the intellectual courage to face the lack of this faith. Apparently the father had made a bad bargain, sacrificing his intellect in the vain hope of shoring up his shaky piety. He "wanted to rest content with faith, but faith broke faith with him," Jung wrote in his "Memories" of the tragedy that befell his father, adding that the "sacrifice of the intellect" commanded by a certain theology is usually rewarded in this shabby manner.

Paul Jung was in his mid-thirties when Carl was born. By the time he reached his forties he was a desolate, broken man. In photos from this period he looked drained, as though his energies were hemorrhaging through a gaping psychic wound. Forced by his ministry to appear more affable in public than he actually felt, he would often act like a querulous child at home. Most of the time, though, a sodden lethargy prevailed. To escape the tiresome provocations of fate, he began to seek solace in books, reading works on psychiatry and hypnotism; but they, too, proved disappointing.[1]

As his gloom deepened, Paul Jung became more of a hypochondriac, forever worried lest he contract *tic douloureux* or stomach cancer. Thus when in the summer of 1895 (he was then fifty-two years old) he began to complain of feeling as though he had stones in his abdomen, he was not taken very seriously by his family and doctor. He sounded too much like the wolf in "Little Red Riding Hood." But in the fall of that year he became bedridden. Visibly wasting under the impact of a disease that turned out to be fatal, he lamented that he had to be carried about the house "like a pile of bones." During his final delirium he wanted to know if his son had passed his doctoral exams. Carl, then a first-year student, replied that everything had gone well. A little while later, Paul Jung died. A merciful lie had marked the end of a life that—if Carl's perception was accurate—had been lived for so long in the shadow of half-truth.

In his "Memories" Carl Jung stressed the weary helplessness

[1]According to some sources, Paul Jung suffered a "nervous breakdown" during this period.

of a father unable to cope with his own perplexities and those of his son. To this querulous sufferer, proud defiance of misfortune was apparently as alien as humble acceptance of it. In his son's portrayal, Paul Jung emerges as a minor-league Job whose faith in God—unlike that of the Biblical hero—did not survive the test of repeated calamities. His unofficial epitaph was spoken by his wife when in Carl's presence she murmured, addressing the empty air: "He died just in time for you." Carl knew exactly what she meant. The father, whose infirm body Carl had lugged around the house during the last illness, had been on the verge of becoming a crushing burden. His timely death unblocked his son's path.

Emilie Jung's unorthodox comment on the death of her husband was not the sort of remark one would expect from the widow of a country minister, who was herself the product of a family of clergymen. Yet while conventional in most matters mundane and spiritual, she was given at times to speaking the unutterable. She had been slim and lovely when she first met Paul Jung, but her disappointing marriage prematurely coarsened her into a stout matron. Too resolute and vital to follow her husband's path of resignation, she turned into a jolly, bustling woman who loved to gossip and complain about her health.

But her facade as a harmless, chatty minister's wife was deceptive. Little Carl was soon to discover behind this front the figure of an alarmingly powerful earth-mother, half sibyl, half witch. This usually submerged figure radiated the "unassailable authority" for which young Carl was yearning and to which he surrendered with ecstacy; but from this figure there also issued something "archaic and ruthless," an aura both sacred and uncanny. Its sacredness, the boy sensed, had little in common with the "merciful God" and the "good Lord Jesus" of his father but emanated from a much darker realm he was to localize later as the sphere of the ancient Germanic worship of Wotan, the Wild Huntsman.

The figure of the mother would undoubtedly have appeared less demonic to the boy if her energies, languishing in her marriage, had not focused too exclusively on him, her oldest surviving—and for nine years, her only—child.[2] To be the focus of his mother's fierce attention imbued Carl with a sense of election but also scorched his budding emotional life. Almost from infancy, Carl felt threatened by cannibalistic forces of uncertain origin. When he was only three or four, he decided that it would be dangerous to let his mother see too much of his inner life; to keep her at bay, he began to build a thick wall of secrecy.

The child would see his mother change abruptly from jovial housewife to pagan seeress. In the midst of the prosaic business of cooking or ironing, she might suddenly get an odd, faraway look and start mumbling strange words, difficult to grasp, seemingly directed at no one, but invariably, once Carl had tuned in, clearly aimed at him, and aimed with an accuracy that struck "to the very core of [his] being."

The sudden transformations made Carl suspect that this ventriloquist mother was actually two separate people who somehow managed to coexist in her ample body. The archaic prophetess was by far the more powerful, awe-inspiring of the two, that much was clear; compared to her, the innocuous housewife was almost larval and unreal. The discovery of his mother's being split in two, of her harboring a second self

[2]The first-born, Paul, had lived only a few days.

concealed from his father's view, alarmed the child. It gave rise to many nightmares. Later, in puberty, Carl was to find that he, too, was split into two people.

This prodigious, double-faced demon-mother, who in her "other" state seemed to traffic with ghosts and spectral presences, did mark her son indelibly. Protectress and witch-Harpy, she established for him the "untrodden, untreadable, nethermost" realm of Faust's Mother-Goddesses as the ultimate reality whose dark womb he craved as his inexpugnable home and at the same time dreaded as voracious black pit.[3]

Growing up between these ill-suited parents whose marriage he later described as a long endurance test, Carl was infected from early on with a deep sense of vulnerability. Throughout his childhood, he was sickly and accident-prone. Once, while crossing a bridge high over the Rhine, he slipped at the edge and came close to falling into the roaring depths below. Years later, as a college student, Carl reflected with a shudder that his early life had been hanging by a thin thread. It struck him as almost miraculous that he had not been "prematurely annihilated." His whole childhood history seemed to him to express "a fatal resistance to life in this world." It was a world he never made.

For one, it was a solitary and narrow world, circumscribed by two unhappy adults. It was also a world that dealt him a series of harsh blows. The shock of these blows, and the sense of exposure and impotence they gave rise to, made him retreat inside himself. He decided early that the inner sanctum, where

[3]Until her dying day, Emilie Jung kept her demonic grip on her son. Shortly before her death when Carl, by then in his late forties and a widely known psychiatrist, was deeply troubled, Emilie suddenly appeared in his study, whispered a few uncannily apposite words, and then vanished as quickly as she had come. Carl Jung, unnerved by her eerie visit, shook like an aspen leaf for hours afterwards.

he could evade or blunt the assaults of fate, alone mattered. Later, rationalizing this feeling, he proclaimed the soul to be the ultimate arbiter of reality, the supreme judge of what befell from without. He overlooked or forgot that it was the external world whose power he was denying that had forced him to turn inward in the first place.

The cruelest blow was his mother's prolonged absence when he was three. An old aunt came to take care of him, but she lacked the mother's "animal warmth." He felt abandoned and cast adrift. Even the prayers his mother had taught him could no longer contain his spreading fears. During the day, he lived in deadly terror of the "Black Man" and the "Man-eater." At night, he had trouble falling asleep and was plagued by bad dreams.

The first of these dreams he remembered was a nightmare that preoccupied him throughout his life. In this dream, he found himself in a vast underground vault, where a tall, trunk-like thing, sitting on a golden throne, towered almost to the arched ceiling. The strange trunk, it turned out, was made of flesh and skin. At the top of its cone-shaped, bald head was a single eye gazing upward. Bathed in an aura of light, the huge shape did not move but somehow gave the impression that it might at any moment crawl off its throne. The thought of this wormlike thing coming toward him filled the dreamer with dread. His terror heightened when he heard his mother's voice, from the outside, warning him that this creepy object was the "man-eater."

This dream of the three- or four-year-old boy was passed on to us, decades after its occurrence, by the octogenarian Jung with the comment that he never told it to anyone until he was in his sixties. Even if the old man's recollection was somewhat flawed, the nightmare of the huge trunk of flesh clearly spot-lighted major life themes. The stony underground vault; the fairy-tale throne; the erect phallus (not recognized as such) cut off from the body and spiritualized by an aura of light; the cannibalistic threat posed by the mobility of the eerie trunk; and, alone among these awesome mysteries, bereft of guardian spirits, the frightened dreamer, whose only link to the outside world is the mother's disembodied voice: these images reflect the anguished bewilderment of a child left to cope on his own with riddles that overtax his mental powers. But one thing Carl grasped even then: he could not tell his parents about his dream. The father, with his brittle good will and his shallow truisms, was poorly equipped to deal with dark enigmas. As for the mother, she was suspect of being in league with the man-eater. The boy felt that he had no choice but to keep his nightmare, later transformed into a revelation, to himself, thus deepening his isolation from his parents. And except for his parents, there was no one in his world. From then on, secrecy, in the form of concealment and mystery, but also of stealth and subterfuge, was to rule his life.

Carl's loneliness became gradually unbearable. He had no playmates. If a visitor of his age happened to stray into his house, he was mocked, fought off, or simply ignored. For weeks on end, Carl played solitary games with ninepins, bricks, and wooden blocks, building tall towers, and then knocking them down with ecstatic frenzy. His pent-up anguish and fury also discharged themselves in countless drawings of war scenes, sieges, bombardments, naval battles. He brooded about ways of making fortresses impregnable and dreamt of becoming a military engineer.

His martial fantasies were interrupted when he started

school at the age of six. At first, Carl was glad to be torn out of his isolation, but his penchant for nasty little pranks did not endear him to his schoolmates. He himself was taken aback by the boastful wildness and malice he often displayed during their games and blamed it on the presence of others; they somehow seemed to estrange him from himself. He felt as if, under the spur of their excitement, a new Carl emerged, strange, fierce, unpredictable. He felt "compelled" to be different from what he thought he was. This change that came about without his agency was scary, and he soon began to retreat from his classmates and the world of the school. The terrors inhabiting his domestic sphere had the advantage of being familiar, at least.

His school shock was followed by further traumas. When he was nine, a sister was born, robbing him of his place as the only child. This event was most unwelcome to him, so distasteful, in fact, that it took him completely by surprise and led him to banish his sister forever after to the most remote corner of his universe. His nervous vigilance had failed to detect the radical changes in his mother's body; and he had asked no questions. When he could no longer ignore what had happened, he was told a story about the stork bringing the baby, which, to this nine-year-old country boy with the carping mind of a Philadelphia lawyer, sounded like humbug. Subsequent odd reactions on his mother's part made him suspect that there was something untoward about this birth. The whole episode left a sour taste and fed his distrust of his parents.

Exiled from his special place within the family, he was soon to suffer another exile: his transfer to the Gymnasium in Basel when he was ten. This move meant a decided turn for the worse in his social fortunes. Among his rustic classmates at primary school he had enjoyed some prestige by virtue of being the minister's son. However, in the eyes of his new fellow-students, most of whom came from well-to-do and status-conscious bourgeois families, the station of a country parson was hardly enviable. Humiliated by the stigmata of poverty and rustic origins, Carl, more of an outcast than ever, sought solace in elaborate secret rituals, cosmological musings, and religious fantasies.

Not only was he an outsider, he was actively disliked by most of his teachers and fellow-students. His teachers viewed him as sly, lazy, and not very bright. There was about him a wary gruffness, and telltale effluvia of a chronic bad conscience, that predestined him for the role of scapegoat. He was accused of plagiarizing, of being underhanded; the misdeeds of others were laid at his door. Even though he deemed most of the accusations unjust, he was usually unable to refute his accusers. At times furious about the unfairness of it all, he was at other times strangely resigned, as if he sensed the workings of a higher justice. His efforts to protect himself were half-hearted and futile. For a while, he resorted to writing down preventive alibis with which he intended to counter future indictments, but these legalistic precautions miscarried.

While his teachers' dislike of him was too militant to be ignored, Carl failed to realize, for some time, *how* unpopular he was with his schoolmates. Self-absorbed and socially naive, he failed at first to pick up the signals of their animosity. Their taunts aimed in his direction usually passed him by, and he made little of the pranks they played at his expense. When the true state of affairs finally dawned on him, he was at a loss to fathom why he was so odious to others. He began to wonder whether he might bear, unknowingly, a Cain-like physical mark. Caught between his teachers' scorn and his classmates' ill will, Carl found his days at school increasingly unbearable.

Then, in early puberty, an unexpected way out presented itself. He was knocked down from behind by a boy and hit his head. This precipitated a series of fainting spells which gave him a respite from the servitude of school. For several months he stayed home, a semi-invalid, brooding, drawing his furious battle scenes, and seeking escape from Man in a romanticized World of Nature, of stones and plants, where "every single thing seemed alive and indescribably marvelous." Later on, he was going to pour his cosmic yearnings into his psychology, his fiction of Man as Cosmos providing an escape from Man.

The doctors were baffled by his fits, diagnosed them as epileptic, prescribed rest and a change of scenery—to no avail. The fainting spells would recur ineluctably whenever Carl opened a textbook. But his initial relief at eluding the torment of school eventually gave way to the fear of losing touch with the everyday world, of becoming a loafer and a vagabond, of no use to himself or others. He accused himself of cowardice, and his guilt feelings, faint at first, were stirred up by the worries about his future he read in his parents' faces. He knew, or thought he knew, that doctors and parents were misdiagnosing his case, that his fainting attacks related to his fear of and distaste for school, that they were, if not exactly contrived, somehow subject to his will. He embarked upon a radical course of action. Resolving not to "give in" any longer to the paralyzing attacks, he grabbed the nearest textbook—and promptly suffered "the finest of fainting fits." But he grimly resumed his reading as soon as he came to, and persisted in his purpose in the face of two further attacks. After an hour or two of this, he felt that his baffling illness—which he later diag-

C. G. Jung—The Haunted Prophet

nosed as a neurosis—had been defeated, and in fact, from then on, the spells abated and gradually disappeared.

Carl exulted at having subdued his invalidism by a sheer act of will. (This experience would markedly affect the ideas of the psychiatrist Jung about the nature of neurosis and may partly account for his somewhat facile therapeutic optimism.) He was able to return to the gymnasium and, by dint of hard work, to improve his grades. In spite of his terror of the abstractions of mathematics, he even managed to get to the top of his class, but being first made him feel so conspicuous that he quickly withdrew to second place. His long absence had made him lose a year, and his joining a new class eased his social situation.

Carl's belief that he was cured, however, was mistaken. To be sure, his heroics had succeeded in erasing the showy hysterical fits, but his anxiety, far from being exorcised, was soon to manifest itself in new, more ominous ways. After a brief interval, the hysteria was followed by an obsessive neurosis with its maddening preoccupations which, in Carl's case, were baroquely religious—and nakedly anal. A fixed idea that drove him to the edge of madness revolved around God sitting on His golden throne high in the sky and smashing with a well-aimed, gigantic turd the freshly painted roof of the Basel cathedral. What made this sort of imagery ominous was the lofty "religious" height from which Carl was viewing his darker impulses. His "flight upward" had started and was proceeding apace.

This flight led him into the realm of self-delusion. He began to feel haunted by "the unity, the greatness, and the superhuman majesty of God." He had tried at first to suppress the tormenting image of God defecating upon His church, but then finally decided that God had set him a test, that the Creator Himself was compelling him to think blasphemous thoughts. When at last, defying hellfire, he yielded to the tabooed thought, he was flooded by a relief so immense that he felt blessed, redeemed, the vessel of Divine Grace. The intensity of his feeling vouchsafed in his eyes that he had encountered the Living God of the prophets. This momentous experience lifted him far above his father and his minister-uncles with their empty, threadbare, and God-forsaken theology. And reading Jung's account of his personal encounter with God, one wonders whether even then he harbored the thought he was to elaborate in his *Answer to Job*, namely, that "homo religiosus," Man-tested-by-God, is morally superior to the Creator who puts him to the test.

Being one of God's Elect did not shield the awkward pread-olescent from further humiliations. In one such moment of ignominy when, crestfallen, he suffered a crude dressing-down from the father of a friend, he was suddenly filled with the conviction that he was actually two persons—the sulky school-boy crushed by a well-deserved scolding, and a powerful, wise old man of the eighteenth century, a man wielding *great authority*, infinitely superior to the fat, boorish manufacturer ranting and raving at him. This conviction of wielding secret power, of being an important personage from a previous century, was fortified by a weird sense of being familiar with the mentality and the utensils of that era. Carl apparently was more pleased than anguished by the emergence of his alter ego. He was to emphasize later that this duality was not a pathological "dissociation." (In a way, he was right; it was more like two conscious selves, dramatized. But he was wrong in asserting, or implying, the "normality" of this kind of cleavage.) As the split became more pronounced, he decided to give names to his two part-selves. Oddly, despite his distaste for the abstractions of

C. G. Jung—The Haunted Prophet

arithmetic, he labeled them Number One (the schoolboy) and Number Two (the wise old man).

Somewhat later, when his father took him to Lucerne and bought him a ticket for the ride to the top of the Rigi mountain (the father shied away from the expense of buying a ticket for himself), Carl, sporting a new English jockey cap and a bamboo cane, was so exalted that he wondered "which was bigger, I or the mountain." And when, toward the end of his high school years, he developed his first systematized daydream, he fancied himself the highest ruler and judge of a medieval town, living inconspicuously in his well-fortified castle, and emerging only now and then "to hold court." But more important than the political power he wielded in his daydream was the fact that the tower of his imaginary castle concealed a great secret known only to him. Inside the tower was a thick copper column whose top, branching into a network of tiny capillaries, drew from the air an ineffable spiritual substance which, condensed and transformed by its passage through the metallic column, would reappear at the bottom as finished gold coins. In his gold-making fantasy, Carl, unlike the medieval alchemists, did not use lead or other base metals for raw material, but something "spiritual" diffused in the air. With his hunger for omens, he was bound to retrospectively view this adolescent daydream as presaging his long-lasting fascination with alchemy in later years. A person of less exalted turn of mind might read the same fantasy as pointing to Jung's future adroitness in extracting money from "spirituality."

In his daydream of the alchemic column Carl fancied himself the discoverer of "a venerable and vital secret of nature," a secret so esoteric that he had to conceal it not only from others, but "in a sense, even from [himself]." Secrecy could go no further. The belief that he was privy to nature's dark mysteries was, as it were, the emotional core of his elaborate daydream. This belief was not limited to his fantasy life. That he knew "things and must hint at things other people do not know, and usually do not want to know," was already for the adolescent Jung the fundamental given of his existence; everything else, even his loneliness, was derivative. He kept alluding to his secret knowledge but felt enjoined from divulging it, presumably because it was beyond the range of people's understanding. In fact, Jung considered it his great achievement *not* to have told what he knew. He viewed Nietzsche's lamentable fate as the inevitable result of baring his innermost vision to a dull, philistine, uncomprehending crowd. Carl Jung was determined to escape this fate. Did he also suspect that the arcane truths revealed to him might be exposed as trivial by the sober light of public scrutiny? If so, he was playing it doubly safe by hinting rather than telling.

This dreamy adolescent, haunted by the sense of his singularity, obsessed with the thought of "belonging to the centuries," rediscovered his own hauntedness everywhere. Feeling homeless in the world of man, he sought refuge in the world of nature—"God's World" he called it—exalting mountains, trees, rivers, plants, and animals. Animals, unlike people, were loyal and trustworthy; plants expressed the playfulness of "God's thought," mountains, its sublime majesty. But nature, too, had its eerie side, encompassing as it did "the darkness of the abyss, the cold impassivity of infinite space and time, and the uncanny grotesqueness of the irrational world of chance." It was the realm of earthquakes, floods, hurricanes and other catastrophes, of the savage wars of species feeding upon each other. And nature was also ghost-haunted. From the early years of his childhood Carl had heard again and again stories of spirits and poltergeists, of second sight and black magic, of witches' Sabbaths on mountaintops, of woods inhabited by revenants, of caves sheltering the elves of night. This ever-present spectral world, which he shared with his seeress-mother, was suffused with an aura of intoxicating awe, with the otherworldly, spine-tingling shimmer of the "numen," as Jung later called it.

A modern, secular word for numen would be "kicks." Carl was a thrill-seeker. During his teens, he was in the grip of one of those swirling, inchoate anxiety states common among middle-class adolescents. This adolescent "storm and stress" typically gives rise to an itch for excitement, for palpitations physical or metaphysical. What was peculiar to Carl Jung was that these preadult sensations stayed with him for decades, that he failed to outgrow the romantic myth of his youth, and that even as an old man he remained committed to the terms of that early struggle.

Haunted from within and without; awed by, and feasting on, his world's portentousness; scorned by people but chosen by God; bookish to the point of caricature, yet impatient with book knowledge; unable to grasp simple problems, yet sensing strange mediumistic gifts in himself; an awkward schoolboy crushed by adult authority but also a powerful dignitary from a previous century: Carl Jung could not resolve these searing contradictions. There was an emptiness at his core, plastered over with self-idolatry, an inner anarchy covered up by a sense of prophetic mission. Lacking a firm identity, Carl felt that things were being done to him, that he was the instrument of higher powers. He kept asking himself, with growing bewilderment: *Who* is doing this to me? *Who* compels me to think these thoughts that I am loath to think? *Who* creates those prescient dreams that far surpass in clarity of vision the perceptions of my conscious mind? Carl Jung's shaky credentials as a citizen of the social world led him to invoke the highest extramundane authority, the "alien guest who comes from both above and below," as the power acting upon, and through, him.

But his sense of prophetic election remained uncertain. Feeling perpetually judged and prejudged by others, he was painfully aware of his lack of a firm inner standard against which to measure himself and his visions. In the face of his parents' psychic disarray, of their failure to validate him, he was in incessant need of self-justification. (His "Memories," where truth subserves myth, were his ultimate attempt to validate himself in the eyes of others, and, precisely because they view his world so single-mindedly from within, a rather compelling attempt.) Few traits were as characteristic of the adolescent Jung as his habit of writing down anticipatory alibis. And it is equally significant that the very old Jung considered the most precious experience of his life a vision that came to him in late manhood where he received the posthumous blessing of his long-dead father.

As he approached the end of high school, Carl's self Number Two with its cosmic aspirations was superseded, for a while, by his self Number One with its practical demands. But the inner split made it difficult to solve practical problems. He agonized over his choice of vocation. Should he become a philosopher, historian, anthropologist, or natural scientist? Floundering back and forth between various fields, unable to locate his main bent (he knew for certain only that he did *not* want to go into theology), he finally sought guidance from his dreams. One dream, in particular, helped to extricate him from the maze of irresolution. In this dream he saw, in the midst of a dark forest, a circular pool surrounded by dense undergrowth. Half-immersed in the water lay a most wondrous creature, a large spherical marine animal, shimmering in opalescent hues, composed of innumerable tiny cells. The dreamer was fascinated by the sight of this magnificent creature lying in its secret, inaccessible place. He felt a keen desire to learn all he could about the secrets of nature. This dream and another, in which he unearthed the bones of prehistoric animals, convinced Jung that he really wanted to study zoology. But zoologists were not much in demand, and as the son of a poor minister Carl had to be practical. Medicine, with its focus on the natural sciences and its promise of a decent income, seemed a sensible compromise. Carl was not entirely happy about having to settle for a compromise. But at the gymnasium he had suffered too many humiliations because of his poverty. And while he viewed his father's shipwreck as caused by a spiritual crisis, he was shrewd enough not to discount the dispiriting effects of an empty purse. Thus in the spring of 1895, Carl Jung registered as a medical student at the University of Basel.

3

GHOSTS

As a young college student, Jung discovered in a friend's library an old booklet on spiritism. Its tales of specters, revenants, and spook intelligences revived memories of his ghost-haunted past. But now, as he read the dusty chronicle of occult happenings, he was struck by the uncanny similarities of apparitions turning up at the most diverse places and eras of history. Perhaps these "supernatural" events, shunned and defamed by science, contained the evidence he had sought all along— evidence of the timeless and spaceless reality of the human soul.

Jung began to read other books on spiritism. He devoured everything on the subject he could find, and he found a great deal. He became fascinated by such men as the nineteenth-century physicist Sir William Crookes, who enlisted the newly discovered technique of photography to assuage his colleagues' skepticism toward his dabbling in the supernatural. Crookes took pictures of a curvaceous lady spirit who had materialized out of thin air before his eyes. To his dismay, even this "tangible proof" failed to sway his obdurate critics. Another spiritist who enthralled Jung was the German poet-physician Justinus Kerner (1786–1862), the discoverer of botulism. Kerner had an encyclopedic knowledge of the medical science of his day. He was content to use its methods as long as they worked. When they failed, he would conclude that he was in the presence of a case of "demonic possession" and turn to hypnosis and exorcism.

One case was that of Friedericke Hauffe, a young woman brought to Kerner in 1826, wasted and delirious. She hallucinated that the dead body of a former love lay in bed with her. Unable to subdue her illness by orthodox methods, Kerner resorted to mesmerism. Under the spell of his hypnotic passes, Friedericke slowly recovered. During her convalescence, she proved to be a highly gifted psychic. Kerner was fascinated by her rich accounts of the spirit world, related in a solemn High German quite at odds with her simple origins. At times, she spoke in an entirely unknown, sonorous language which, according to her, was mankind's original tongue, long extinct. Kerner took her into his house, observed her at close range, and, after her death, published his observations in a book, *The Seeress of Prevorst*. He saw her mediumistic feats as proof of "the insertion of a Spirit World into our universe."

And that is exactly what Jung inferred from Kerner's report. He practically learned the book by heart, and airily dismissed the possibility that Kerner had been hoodwinked by a clever hysteric. While musing over Friedericke's revelations, he made the providential discovery that a young relative of his, Helene Preiswerk, was a medium. He decided to attend her seances, and later made her the subject of his doctoral thesis.

In his thesis, Jung tried to disguise Helene's identity, calling her "S.W." She was a cousin on his mother's side, whose family history sheds a curious light on Jung's own genetic heritage. In fact, Jung introduced S.W. as "a girl with poor inheritance"; her numerous family seemed to consist mostly of bizarre characters, tottering on the edge of madness. Trances, visions, hallucinations, and prophetic mutterings were, so to speak, the daily diet of the Preiswerks. Helene was a slight, fragile creature with pale skin. Her piercing stare had a paranoid quality, but otherwise she seemed unremarkable. Having lost her father in early childhood, she found herself at the mercy of a coarse mother who treated her as a drudge. When she was fifteen, she attended some spiritistic meetings where tables were raised. The whole affair seemed an amusing game to her until her talent as a medium was discovered. Formerly a mere extra, she soon became the star performer of her circle.

Helene's career as a medium started with table-turning. But she quickly proceeded to weightier matters. Her first prop was a "psychograph," an upside-down wine glass, which spelled out messages from the beyond by moving with lightning speed to letters of the alphabet arranged on a table. Impatiently, she soon dropped the scurrying wine glass to become her own psychograph. Pale as a ghost, her eyes closed, hardly breathing, she would slowly sink into a chair and stiffen. Then she would begin to speak: spirit messages from people long dead, using her cataleptic body as a channel, flowed easily from her almost motionless lips. Gradually, these trances evolved into full-fledged psycho-drama. She began to orchestrate her utterances with bold gestures, throwing herself into attitudes of rapt prayer, rising to dizzy heights of rhetoric. During such moments of rapture she said that her soul was joined to her body by a tenuous thread.

At first it was mainly the spirit of Samuel Preiswerk, Helene's (and Jung's) grandfather, who spoke through her. She had not known him personally, but according to those who had, she rendered him with uncanny acumen, matching to perfection the pompous and solemn tone of his sermons. Samuel's messages from the beyond were dishearteningly trite and edifying —spiritistic commercials. Apparently, death and after-life had failed to affect or change him. From his supernatural pulpit, he kept mouthing the same platitudes he had perpetrated on his parishioners during his lifetime.

From the very start, Helene took her encounters with the spirit world as a matter of course, as if her whole past had been preparing her for the calling of medium. She never gave any sign of doubting the reality of her visions. When Jung taunted her that her spirits might be delusions, sick products of a sick brain, she replied with quiet dignity that she could not tell whether the spirits really were the people they claimed to be. "But that my spirits exist," she said, "is beyond all doubt. I see them in front of me, I can touch them. I speak with them about everything I want, as naturally as I am speaking with you today. They must be real." Jung, who had played devil's advocate, inwardly agreed.

Helene's spreading fame as a medium aroused the envy of her three sisters. They, too, began to have visions; but, discriminated against by the spirits, they could not match Helene's feats which became increasingly extravagant. After hearing about the Seer of Prevorst, she began to do self-hypnotic

exercises, drawing odd figure-eights with her arms in the unre-
sisting air. Like the seer, she began to speak in an unknown
exotic tongue. Genteel spirits, with high-sounding names, favored her increasingly with their presence and gave her seances
an aristocratic cachet. First, one Ulrich von Gerbenstein made
his appearance, a gossip and raconteur, whose particulars remained vague. He was followed by two ladies of rank: Elizabeth
von Thierfelsenburg and Berthe de Valours. Most inappropri-
ately, a commoner, the dead brother of a man present at
Helene's sessions, intruded into this select company. While
holding forth on brotherly love, this spirit flirted in a most
unspiritual way with some ladies of the circle. His stale compliments and silly jokes were duly criticized as most unbecoming
for his station, whereupon he withdrew in a huff.

To deflect attention from this unworthy spirit, Helene revealed that she was privileged in the spirit realm and had a
special spiritual name: Ivenes. As Ivenes she went on long trips
to visit dead relatives or to venture "into the space between the
stars" with its "countless spirit worlds." On these trips into
galactic space, she had learned a great deal about the metaphysics of the beyond. According to her, the forces governing the
universe were arranged in seven concentric circles. She dictated to Jung a complex scheme of this system of forces, labeling each of the spheres with ornate Latinized names. If the
visible world *appears* to be so sharply divided from the beyond,
she said, it is only because of man's defective sense organs. In
reality, the transition is gradual. Hence some human beings,
endowed with perfect senses, can see events invisible to the rest
of mankind.

Ivenes was also remarkably well informed about the genealo-
gies of various spirits and their numerous rebirths. Being rein-

carnated at least every two hundred years (unlike minor spirits who were reborn less often), Ivenes had been Elizabeth von Thierfelsenburg and Madame de Valours in her earlier lives. During the eighteenth century, she had been a simple preacher's wife in Germany, but with an uncommon fate: she was seduced by the great Goethe and bore him a son (who, according to the Jungian family legend, could have been Carl Jung's grandfather). As Madame de Valours she had given birth to an earlier incarnation of Carl Jung and was subsequently burned as a witch. The shock of this event persuaded her son to become a monk. Over the centuries, Ivenes's relish for frequent rebirths, and men's insatiable appetite for her, had given rise to a huge, tortuous family tree. Altogether the past of the Preiswerks as revealed by Ivenes was replete with horrors: deaths by poison, knifings, seduction and rape, incest, and the falsifying of wills. Ivenes was especially hard on a pretty young woman who was also a relative of Jung. She accused her of being the reincarnation of a notorious French poisoner who had prospered under the reign of Louis XVI and who even in her present life continued her deadly trade. Among her victims were her husband and her brother both of whom she had dispatched, the latter after an incestuous affair. Jung was taken aback by this baroque list of accusations, but failed to recognize that it was inspired by jealousy.

Helene's career as a medium ended rather abruptly when she was caught in a flagrant deception. She had tried to fake a materialization by throwing about a few objects she had hidden in her clothing. Her exposure led to her leaving for Paris to become a dressmaker, a more material occupation. When Jung visited her there, he found her unwilling to talk about her experiences as a psychic. She died of tuberculosis, at the young age of twenty-six. From her precocity as a child, she had flowered to a bright maturity in her last years. But during her final illness, her adult self unraveled so that she had reverted to the stage of a child by the time she died.

His cousin's spiritistic seances made a deep impression on Carl Jung. That she had been caught in a fraudulent act in the end shook his faith in Helene's integrity, but not his belief in the reality, and the transcendent meaning, of the events he had observed. He was well aware of the fact that most mediums have hysteric personalities, and that hysterics are prone to use subterfuges when their natural powers to "make an impression" prove defective. That Helene had stooped to one or more acts of deception did not imply that her earlier feats had been faked. That she herself was unable to sustain her initial faith in the genuineness of the supernatural events that had been channeled through her body did not mean that Jung had to follow her upon this treacherous path. In fact, in later years, he called these seances "the great experience which superseded my whole early philosophy." Far from feeling duped by paranormal oddities of questionable authenticity, he was certain that he had learned "something objective" about the human soul. But at the time he was not ready to weave these amazing experiences into a larger system.

In his doctoral thesis, supervised by the sober Eugen Bleuler, Jung showed great "scientific" caution. Ignoring the deeper import of the events he described, he was content to give a mere *psychological* analysis of the case of Helene P. In this ill-fitting stance of the detached clinician, Jung focused in particular on the changes in Helene's character during her trances, the alternations of Helene Preiswerk and Ivenes. Their interplay reminded Jung of his own two-soul split into Number One and Number Two.

Comparing Helene's metamorphoses with earlier cases of

dual selves, Jung noted that, as a rule, self Number Two is the psychological opposite, or negative, of self Number One. A typical instance was Mary Reynolds, an American girl who after a deep sleep lasting twenty hours had completely forgotten her past. Upon awakening, she no longer recognized her family. Her personality and way of life were completely changed. Formerly a rather melancholy woman, she was now cheerful, even boisterous; previously shy, she had become outgoing to the point of being saucy; from a homebody, she was transformed into a madcap roaming on horseback through woods and mountains. After five weeks of this nomad life, she again fell into a deep sleep, coming to as her first self. These two states of Mary's personality alternated for a while, until her second self finally gained the upper hand.

With Helene Preiswerk, matters were different. Her trance personality was less the negative than the exaltation of her usual self. Ivenes was sublime where Helene was hysterical; she was composed, bright, and articulate where the other was flighty, dull, and awkward. In short, Ivenes was Helene glorified. The almost saintly perfection of Ivenes made Jung the clinician feel ill at ease. There was something contrived about her ways, something overdone about her "act." Yet her playacting could not be called a matter of conscious deceit; genuine in its contrivance, it radiated the good faith of the hysteric who is true in the midst of her falsehood. At least, that is how Jung saw her. To bolster his point he cited, for the first time, Sigmund Freud whose newly coined concept of "hysterical identification" seemed to fit Ivenes to perfection. If Freud was right, Ivenes's fitful existence represented an unconscious fulfillment of repressed wishes, an acted-out dream.

This thesis seemed to be borne out by the medium's elaborate family myths with their black-and-white antagonists: Ivenes, the epitome of goodness, and the wicked poisoners who revel in murder, adultery, and incest. But Ivenes, too, has her sexual side; she is, after all, the great mother, the prodigious womb with her innumerable offspring. Hence Jung was led to conclude, in a Freudian vein, that Ivenes's protracted daydream was indeed of a sexual nature. But having granted that much, Jung had to delve further. What about the other part-selves that had emerged during Helene's trances? What was their psychological significance? They were in the main of two types, represented by the edifying grandfather and the foppish von Gerbenstein. In Jung's view, these two types stood for polar sides of Helene's personality which she could not integrate in her conscious life. The appearance of the spirits signaled this lack of synthesis, but also the attempt of the strangled self to realize its true potential. This unremitting drive to overcome the inner split bore witness to the existence of a guiding agent, an affirmative psychic force. Thus, Jung asserted, the occult events of spiritism yield evidence of the reality of the soul.

At the time he wrote his thesis, Jung did not dwell upon the reality of the soul. Cautious to the point of being timorous, he restricted himself to viewing Helene's spirits through the reductive lenses of the pathologist. Only rarely, fleetingly, did the later Jung emerge. He did so for a brief moment when he cited an author who saw hallucinations as "harbingers and also signs of an immense spiritual power," fully compatible with "the most perfect health of mind and body." Jung did not say then whether he agreed with such heretical notions. But the fascination with spiritism that Helene Preiswerk had aroused led him to take part, twenty-five years later, in another series of seances, sponsored by a German investigator whose name could have been invented by Ivenes: Albert Baron von Schrenck-Notzing.

An aristocrat and physician, descended from a family of aristocratic physicians, von Schrenck-Notzing had come to the study of the occult via his experiments with hypnosis. Despite his prestigious name and his irreproachable academic credentials, he was taxed with being a charlatan by most of his German colleagues. Only after gaining some recognition in England and France was he taken more seriously in his own country. In the early 1920s, one could observe "university professors, and not only philosophers and psychologists, but natural scientists, physicists, physiologists and medical men, who take advantage of the bad street-lighting in Munich to steal like conspirators to the evening sittings of Herr von Schrenck-Notzing to see what it does not profit them to see. For they must know, and they do, that the only way of remaining intact (in their skepticism) is to shut their eyes and not see."

These lines about the clandestine vogue of spiritism among members of the scientific guild were written by Thomas Mann who himself had participated in a few seances at the Baron's palatial Munich residence. Mann noted that, after witnessing such a demonstration, some inveterate skeptics had grown "very cautious in their skepticism." A somewhat "lax and benevolent" skeptic himself, Thomas Mann felt queasy and "slightly seasick," overcome by "profound wonderment with a tinge, not of horror, but of disgust," when he saw the feats performed by the medium Willy S., "a dentist by profession and a devil of a fellow in the psychical line." Before his "uncorrupted eyes," Mann watched a handkerchief lifted from the floor by what appeared to be a disincarnated hand, rising "with a swift, assured, vital, almost beautiful movement . . . out of the shadow into the rays of light, which colored it reddish . . . it was manipulated from the inside, by some living thing, compressed, shaken, made to change its shape, in the two or three seconds it was held up in the lamplight. Then moving with the same quiet assurance, it returned to the floor."

Thomas Mann felt certain that in the experiments he witnessed, sleight-of-hand and trickery were humanly impossible. (He himself acted as a control, holding the medium's hands during his telekinetic performance.) Trained experimenters, like the French scholar Gustave Geley, agreed. The latter stated categorically after a similar session: "I do not merely say that there was no deception present in these sittings; I say that the possibility of deception was ruled out." Much as he would have liked to discount what he had seen, to dismiss it as a clever trick, Mann found it impossible to do so. He felt thrown into a "maddening" state of mind where reason commanded him "to recognize what reason on the other hand would reject as impossible."

No such conflict was set off in Jung by Schrenck-Notzing's experiments. Jung's philosophy, by that time, was catholic and rubbery enough to accommodate the most outlandish phenomena. And yet, in his utterances to others, Jung was oddly ambiguous regarding his own attitude toward the paranormal. He agreed with those who, like Freud, denounced the inanity and triteness of most alleged communications from the spirit world. When his former schoolmate, the philosopher Paul Häberlin, told Jung to his face that he, Jung, was much too intelligent to believe all the mystical nonsense he had published, Jung seemed to concur. "Mundus vult decipi" (Mankind wants to be deceived), he lamely replied. But after

C. G. Jung—The Haunted Prophet

Schrenck-Notzing's death, Jung told the latter's research assistant that he was convinced of the genuineness of the spiritistic phenomena he had witnessed. When asked why he did not say so in public, Jung became evasive. There were so many other important things he had to convey and which people were reluctant to accept. To prematurely state his belief in paranormal events would further compromise him and his unpopular cause.

When he was well into his seventies, Jung detailed in a letter to a Swiss theologian some of his ideas about paranormal events.[1] The letter dealt with the enigma of the legendary Swiss saint, Brother Klaus, of whom it was said that for twenty years of his life he had touched neither food nor drink. Jung accepted as a fact, "corroborated by reliable witnesses," that the twenty-year fast had actually taken place. While not sure how to account for this miracle, he gave some hints about the direction in which an explanation might be sought. Jung cited the case of a medium, known to him, who produced ectoplasmic phenomena. In Jung's presence, an electrical engineer had measured the degree of ionization in the vicinity of the medium's body. He found that ion formation was sixty times greater than normal at the point where the ectoplasmic emanation had occurred, but was normal near the other areas of the medium's body. In the face of these curious findings, Jung thought it "conceivable that persons in the vicinity of the medium might act as a source of ions—in other words, nourishment might be effected by the passage of living albumen from one body to another." On such slender empirical foundations did Jung build his hypotheses about the mechanics of paranormal events.

[1]This letter was published in revised form in *Neue Wissenschaft* (Olten and Fribourg, 1950/51).

It is typical of Jung that he turned to an electrical engineer to legitimize the paranormal. The natural sciences provided for him the ultimate touchstone of reality, and the major avenue to an explanation of the occult. His naive faith in the solidity of the reality articulated by science (by which he mainly meant natural science) marked him as a child of the nineteenth century; so did his attempts to *prove* the existence, and *explain* the possibility, of the paranormal by integrating it into this *scientific* world view. Despite his revolutionary posturings, Jung was at bottom an intellectual (and political) conservative. He had neither the stomach nor the mental equipment to seriously question the arrogant claim of the natural sciences to define the borderlines of reality.

Since it did not occur to Jung to deny the legitimacy of this claim, his attempts to vindicate the paranormal had to rely upon the rules of evidence formulated by the exact sciences. Hence his excitement was great when he heard of the experiments of J. B. Rhine who studied extrasensory perception in the laboratory and validated his findings by means of statistical analysis. Jung apparently saw nothing incongruous in enlisting the methodology of experimental physics to verify paranormal phenomena the very occurrence of which constituted a radical challenge to the reality articulated by early twentieth-century science. Why did Jung fail to recognize this challenge? Largely because he was too preoccupied with his personal vendetta against the threadbare theology of his father and uncles. His zeal to topple their shopworn idols blinded him to the real idols of his era—the electrons, protons, neutrons, and other elementary particles promulgated by the Rutherfords, de Broglies, Diracs, Plancks, Heisenbergs, Bohrs, and their successors. Led astray by his crusading spirit, he failed to see that his efforts to validate spiritualist phenomena piecemeal, and within the

C. G. Jung—The Haunted Prophet

physicalistic framework familiar to him, were bound to fail. This framework by its very nature could not accommodate paranormal phenomena. In order to survive, it had to consign them to the limbo of the occult.

Only the radical breakup of this scientistic frame of reference could lead to the validation of the paranormal. While more beholden to the scientism of the nineteenth century than he realized, Jung furthered the process of its erosion. His visionary (and quixotic) preoccupations emphasized the necessity to redefine reality in such a way as to make it more hospitable to what passed in Jung's time—and passes even now—for paranormal.

4

THE SENSE OF
NON-SENSE

In December 1900, the twenty-five-year-old Jung joined the
Burghölzli asylum in Zurich as psychiatric intern. A photo
from this period shows an athletic-looking young man with stiff
collar and steel-rim glasses, a little moustache, short-cropped,
already receding hair, and the beginnings of a paunch; he is
hiding his hands behind his back, and his distrust behind a
thin, supercilious smile. The impression one gets is of a rough-
edged loner. And that is apparently how he struck his new
colleagues. They found him aloof, arrogant—and full of fascinating ideas.

The director of the Burghölzli at the time was Eugen
Bleuler, one of the first hospital psychiatrists to introduce into
his clinic some of the new, largely unproven ideas of Sigmund

Freud. Bleuler was almost fanatically dedicated to his work and courteous to a fault. During his early years at the Burghölzli, he would insist on personally carrying the suitcases of newly arrived assistants to their quarters at the hospital. Like Freud, whom he resembled in his diffident manner, Bleuler had an unusually expressive burning gaze. It reflected an intense spiritual fire, but also deep inner strife. Bleuler's personality was —to use a present-day term—schizoid. Completely alive at one moment, he would suddenly, without warning, fade into some private void. Heavy-handedness and dictatorial airs were foreign to him. He simply took it for granted that his assistants worked just as hard as he did.

When Jung came to the Burghölzli, its medical staff consisted of four psychiatrists (including Bleuler); they were in charge of about four hundred patients. Jung experienced Burghölzli as a "secular cloister" with oppressively narrow horizons. He spoke of the "unending desert of routine" circumscribing his daily life. In his meager spare time he buried himself in psychiatric books and journals. He also somehow managed to compile some secret statistics on the genetic background of his Swiss colleagues. This hobby expressed Jung's continued scorn for his peers (also his concern about his own heredity); it was the more piquant in that Bleuler's sister and other members of his family suffered from chronic mental illness.

The relationship between Jung and Bleuler was difficult from the outset. In some ways it was a preview, on a smaller scale, of Jung's stormy dealings with Freud. At first, there was a honeymoon period, fairly brief in this case. Already Jung's acknowledgment in his thesis of Bleuler's support sounded rather stiff. (He mentioned that Bleuler lent him some books.)

But in Jung's comments about his chief during the first years of their collaboration a note of respect prevailed. The picture changed gradually. By the end of 1902, when Jung went to study with Pierre Janet in Paris, he was already disillusioned with Bleuler. A few years later, Jung would describe him in a letter to Freud as someone "who for many years was a frosty old bachelor," forced to "do a lot of repressing in his life."

From then on his scorn for his once revered chief became increasingly outspoken. He would accuse Bleuler of having "insuperable resistances" to analyzing his dreams, of being pusillanimous in his distaste for the word "auto-eroticism." (At the same time, Jung himself was allergic to the term "libido.") By the end of 1907, Bleuler had become in Jung's eye "the most notable example of a brilliantly successful pseudo-personality"; a few months later, a man "festooned with complexes from top to bottom." Eventually, he was stripped of all competence in matters psychoanalytic; even the basics of Freud's theories eluded him, if his assistant was to be believed.

Only rarely Jung had a good word to say about Bleuler during those years. Thus, at one point, he lauded Bleuler's "magnificent Zurich open-mindedness." (This probably in a moment of disenchantment with Freud's less than open-minded attitude.) But mostly, Jung's vocabulary with regard to his chief expressed rage and deprecation. In 1910, Jung was incensed at Bleuler's refusal to join the Psychoanalytic Society. To Jung, this meant "war," but it turned out to be an undeclared war: Jung had to wait for an opportunity to take his "revenge." When the break with Bleuler, long in the making, finally occurred, it was neither sharp nor definite; some sort of professional intercourse survived. Yet Jung was more hurt than he had expected.

C. G. Jung—The Haunted Prophet

In his autobiography Jung failed to mention Bleuler even once. This omission was quite a feat. Jung seemed to have completely erased from his memory the unselfish teacher to whom he owed a great deal intellectually and who had so generously smoothed his path. But, then, gratitude toward fatherly sponsors was never one of Jung's strong points.

In 1900, though, when Jung entered the worldly cloister of the Burghölzli, he was ready to emulate his chief. Following Bleuler's example, he spent long hours with individual patients, listening intently to their ideas, however outlandish. It was not Jung's nature to be merely a passive listener, and he would inject himself quite forcefully into these interviews. With many schizophrenics, in particular, he found it easy to make contact. Psychotics given to outbursts of physical violence did not scare him. One day, an old friend was making the rounds with Jung, when of a sudden he saw a fist flying through the air, barely missing him. An upset patient had tried to practice a knock-out blow on the visitor. The friend was duly alarmed, but Jung, unruffled, broke out into a loud neighing laugh, explaining that this amateur boxer was noted for his magnificent uppercuts.

Jung's initial interest in his clinical work was theoretical rather than practical. He wanted to observe "how the human mind reacts to the sight of its own destruction," implying that this destruction was wrought primarily by physical causes. And he hoped that, by studying psychic "deviations from so-called normality," he would learn something definite about the nature of the human soul. His coworkers might mock his preoccupations as quaint, but Jung was increasingly certain that the notion of "soul" not only designated something real, but was the most basic, the most *realistic* concept of psychology.

To Jung, these philosophical issues bore directly on his work as a psychiatrist. They led him to explore with painstaking care the life-stories of his patients. In doing so, he discovered much that remained hidden from his colleagues. That the doctor's probing into the patient's past might shed light on his psychosis, and might even prove therapeutic, was then anything but the truism it has become by now. On the contrary, such an idea was akin to heresy. But Jung's talks with his charges convinced him that to clarify their opaque past meant to make sense out of the non-sense of their madness. The self-willed young doctor soon made use of new, unrecognized methods to test this belief.

In particular, Jung put an old psychological test to new uses: the word-association test. This test is based upon the notion that the linkage ("association") of contiguous ideas is the basic anabolic process of the human mind. The test procedure is to read a list of words to the subject, who responds with the first words that come to mind. The reaction time of each response is measured.

Before Jung, psychiatrists were content to register superficial differences between the test responses of normal and disturbed people. From these they hoped to obtain diagnostic cues. Jung, however, gave the test a new depth. He saw and explored its potential to become a sort of divining rod for the discovery of unconscious ideas. This meant that, in a most unexpected way, he brought about a rapprochement between experimental psychology and Freud's psychoanalysis, whose main thrust at the time was the laying bare of the unconscious through dream analysis. This association between laboratory psychology and the Freudian science, brokered by Jung's piercing the unconscious with the solid apparatus of exact measurements, pro-

C. G. Jung—The Haunted Prophet

vided psychoanalysis with some of the academic respectability it needed or thought it needed; it also improved the reputation of the evanescent, scientifically suspect realm of dreams. If the unconscious could be tapped by means of stopwatches and statistical coefficients, then perhaps it was real. For reality, to those who put their faith in so-called exact science, is the experimentally verifiable.

When he began experimenting with word associations, Jung had already read Freud's *Interpretation of Dreams*. Increasingly he accepted Freud's notion that "repressed" life fragments— that is, experiences which have not been consciously assimilated—play a major role in mental illness. Jung thus made the Freudian idea his own: the meaning of psychic symptoms is the history of their origins. To this hypothesis, Jung gave his personal stamp. Himself secretive to the core, he wanted to uncover his patients' "guilty secret" that corroded their psychic life. Unlike the basic Freudian trauma, the Jungian secret is not necessarily infantile or sexual; contrary to the trauma, it is conscious or half-conscious; it owes its mischievous power to its owner's crabbed resolve to cling to it. Thus the conscious evasion of truth, as much as the unconscious lie of repression, was seen by Jung as pathogenic. The Jungian neurotic began to resemble Dostoievski's pale sinner rather than Freud's Gulliver ensnared by the inexorable mechanisms of defense.

Jung was able to show that the words from the association list to which a test subject reacted in a disturbed way could be easily grouped around a few emotionally charged themes. These traumatic "complexes," as they were called, might involve conscious secrets or unconscious memories; in either case, they were invariably brought to light, as if by black magic, by the Jungian analysis of the association test. It turned out that the contents of these affective complexes were usually pretty much the same for normal people and neurotics, but that the latter were plagued by a larger number, and a greater intensity, of these overcharged themes.

Jung's use of the association test made him appear to be an uncanny mind-reader who could lift, with the greatest ease, anxiously guarded secrets from his patients; in doing so, he often produced a healing catharsis. But if Jung was so effective as a mind-reader, it was largely because many patients wanted, unconsciously or even consciously, to have their minds read, wanted someone to *guess* their crushing secret. Jung did not allow enough for this silent complicity—with the result that he overestimated the test's (or his own) perspicacity. When he later used the test as a guilt-detector, to track down the authors of some petty crimes, he did not pay sufficient heed, initially, to the distinction between displaced neurotic guilt attached to imaginary misdeeds, and simple guilt stemming from specific criminal acts.

The association test proved also useful in probing the chaotic inner world of schizophrenics. It was able to detect in them, too, deep-rooted, intensely charged feelings. But the exposure of their complexes did not lead to tangible improvement with schizophrenics, as it often did with neurotics. From this Jung concluded that the personalities of schizophrenics were far more splintered than those of neurotics, and their complexes more autonomous; the latter existed, so to speak, on their own, and were hard to influence. This, at least, was Jung's opinion at the time.

Still, Jung managed to go further than to simply demonstrate that schizophrenics were riddled with complexes. The association test enabled him to decode the hidden meaning of

C. G. Jung—The Haunted Prophet

the seemingly abstruse babbling of schizophrenics. He succeeded in showing that there is a kernel of meaning in the most amorphous "word salad," that the right questions lend sense to delusions, and that, after all, the convoluted, alien language of the insane can be deciphered like an old Egyptian hieroglyph.

Jung's proof that the language of insanity, far from being meaningless, is a sense within non-sense was a radical step in psychiatry. It bared the weakness of the accepted dogma that all mental illness is organic, a result of brain disorder. Psychiatrists, till then intent upon treating only the somatic "substratum" of mental disorders, mostly ignored the psychic "secondary symptoms" of these disturbances. Jung himself, at the time and later, never seriously disputed the possibility or likelihood of a somatic basis of schizophrenia. His demonstration, however, that psychological factors play a large role in its genesis and symptomatology undermined psychiatry's dogmatic assumptions about mental disorder and paved the way for later radical departures from these one-dimensional views.

The case of Babette S. was Jung's prize example of the disclosure of psychotic delusions through psychological analysis. The patient, born in 1845, was an unmarried dressmaker from a poor family. She became ill at the age of thirty-nine, "on the threshold of the age," Jung observes, "when so many dreams are brought to naught." Rapidly progressing delusions and hallucinations led to her being committed to an asylum. When Jung first noticed her, she had already been at Burghölzli for more than fifteen years. Her speech, when delusional, had become completely unintelligible. She launched forth with combinations of words that made sense to no one. She said, for example, that she was "the Bank-Note Monopoly." She also laid claim to being "Socrates" or "the finest professorship and the finest world of arts." At other times she called herself "Maria Stuart," "the Lorelei," or "Germania and Helvetia of exclusively sweet butter."

Jung's colleagues recognized Babette's paranoia and megalomania but were completely baffled by her mad twaddle. Yet Jung spared no pains in tracking down, with the help of association techniques, the meanings buried in her strange utterances. And he actually managed to find in them a comprehensible pattern. Thus, her assertion that she was Socrates meant that she, Babette, was suffering the same fate as Socrates, who was slandered and forced to die in prison. Bad people had unjustly imprisoned her, who "had never cut a thread" unnecessarily, making her another "Maria Stuart." Her less transparent declarations that she was the finest professorship and the finest world of arts referred once more to her superior work as a seamstress: she felt like a professor or artist in her vocation. She made only the best clothing and called it by the bizarre neologism: "snail-museum-clothes."

Babette's repeated assertions that she was "the Monopoly" and "the Queen of Orphans" could also be deciphered. With "the Monopoly," she meant the monopoly of printing money which she believed herself to own and with which she could create immense riches for herself, to make up for the wretchedness of her life in the asylum. "The Queen of Orphans" alluded to the fact that her parents had died early, in great poverty; but since her ownership of "the Monopoly" put her in possession of uncounted treasures, which she could share with her parents, she was also rich like a queen—the Queen of Orphans.

Jung's careful decoding of the apparently chaotic, unstructured hodgepodge of Babette's speech showed that there was a human being with a potentially rich inner life hiding behind the imbecilic, larvalike behavior of the chronic schizophrenic. Unfortunately, the personal core of Babette S. was too overgrown with delusions to be reached by therapy—or so Jung thought at the time. But his inability to help the poor seamstress did not cloud his achievement of devising a method to explore the psychological meaning of psychosis.

In 1905, Jung was appointed lecturer in psychiatry at the University of Zurich. His first topics were clinical psychiatry and psychotherapy; later he also offered courses on psychoanalysis and the psychology of primitive peoples. Jung was to teach at the university for eight years, without rising above his original rank of *Privatdozent*. When he resigned in 1913, pleading a heavy workload, his colleagues thought that his real reason for leaving was his lack of prospects for promotion. Even if they were wrong, Jung was undoubtedly bitter toward the university that failed to recognize his genius. About forty-five years later, when he was eighty-two, that lack of recognition still rankled: at that time he complained in a letter to a Japanese admirer that his teachings had progressed far too slowly in their journey toward acceptance; not only had they taken several decades to reach Japan, but they had yet to enter the doorway of the university of his own city!

But if *Privatdozent* Jung was misprized by his own countrymen, he found ready recognition abroad. Through his studies in word association, conducted with the help of American coworkers and published in part in American journals, Jung became known quite early in the United States. His peculiar blend of depth psychology and experimental technique appealed to the pragmatism of American psychiatrists who soon began to refer patients to him. The later Jung who forswore exact measurement, and was shaman, mystic, pundit, and prophet rolled into one, touched the Emersonian chord in the American character. Jung's growing prestige as a therapist, writer, and spokesman of a new school did the rest. No matter how superficial the reasons for Jung's renown with Americans —and English people—may have been, the influx of "Anglo-Saxon" patients grew until Jung's clientele was recruited largely from two, partly overlapping categories: Anglo-Saxons and women.

Jung's magnetism for female neurotics of all shades was remarkable; it became irresistible if such women happened to be British or American. Part of Jung's secret was that he empathized strongly with the aspirations of women who were or felt misunderstood; undoubtedly, his extreme, almost "feminine" sensitivity also contributed to this peculiar sex-appeal. In any case, women were his first, most enthusiastic, and most fanatic disciples. In Zurich medical circles, these overly rapturous devotees were tagged with the inevitable label, "Jung-Frauen."

In the early years of his practice, Jung felt pretty helpless before the therapeutic demands of his patients. Psychotherapy was then mainly exorcism; it tried to remove neurotic symptoms by adjuring them, via hypnosis and suggestion, to go away. The results of such blandishments were uncertain and usually not long-lasting. As we have seen, Jung soon discovered that many neurotics were laboring under the burden of anxiously kept secrets which were obviously related to their mental suffering. These secrets isolated the sufferer from others and poisoned his mind. If Jung somehow managed to divine the secret or induced the patient to part with it, the beneficial effect of such an exposure was unmistakable; quite often it was long-lasting.

C. G. Jung—The Haunted Prophet

Those suffering from conscious or half-conscious secrets were mostly hysterics. But there was another large group of neurotics, labeled "asthenics" by Jung.[1] With them, the category of personal secrets seemed to play only a minor, if any, role; a pervasive, wholly automatic secretiveness marked, and distorted, their entire life-style. Their trademark was the radical erasure of their most crucial feelings. To undo such wholesale repression was much more difficult than lifting his secret from a half-willing hysteric. In these cases, Jung tried to apply Freudian techniques of free association and dream analysis. He found, however, that Freud's methods promised more in theory than they were able to achieve in practice. Also Jung could not accept the Freudian emphasis on early sexual traumata as crucial to the genesis of any neurosis. Jung's rejection of this Freudian premise may have been determined more by his personality—with its almost instinctive distaste for the "darker" sides of sexuality—than by factual evidence in this matter. After his break with Freud, Jung even proclaimed that the Freudian wallowing in the sexual aspects of human life was bound to derail the process of therapy.

As Jung gained in experience, he became more distrustful of all psychological theorizing about therapy. Theories aspire to universal validity; they abstract from the individual, the focus of therapeutic concern. Gradually, Jung came to believe that good therapy, like a good suit—and a good religious credo—has to be tailor-made. The therapist who clings to the dictates of theory and wants to heal "by the book" betrays by this very fact his inadequacy. What ultimately matters in therapy, according to Jung, is the readiness of the analyst to fully enter

[1] Today they would be diagnosed as obsessive or depressive.

into the psycho-drama enacted by the patient. A too rigorous division of roles, a too forceful assertion of medical authority, is apt to abort the therapeutic process. Only the therapist willing to shed his personal defenses can deeply affect his therapeutic partner. If the therapist lends himself to such exposure, it is because he himself is wounded or vulnerable. "Only the wounded physician heals." Only he who is prepared to change himself can transform those frozen by neurotic fixations. These and similar statements summarize some of the notions about psychotherapy which Jung gradually evolved during his early years of practice. That he professed such attitudes does not mean necessarily that he could live up to them. Jung was less capable of stripping himself of his defenses than he liked to think.

Jung's belief that he had to improvise a new therapy for each patient often led to quite unorthodox measures on his part. Thus, with one of his early American patients, a compulsive tippler, Jung resorted to a bit of trickery to produce a desired result. This man was an executive in a firm owned by his domineering mother. He drank too much to numb his humiliating awareness of being under his mother's thumb. Jung advised him to leave his job in order to free himself, but this he could not summon the courage to do. Whereupon Jung went behind the patient's back and wrote his mother that he was an irresponsible alcoholic, who ought to be fired. The mother obliged. Of course, the son was furious at Jung when he found out what had happened, but after his belated ouster from the maternal nest proceeded to make a brilliant career. Jung's subterfuge was thus justified by its happy results, at least in his own eyes. Later Jung was to use similar measures to induce hibernating artists (among them, reputedly, James

Joyce) to get back in harness. One is struck by Jung's penchant for pulling strings and rearranging life situations in order to force psychic growth.

But clever dodges are no substitute for honest analytical work, and apparent short cuts to psychic health are apt to turn into dead ends. While Jung could not always resist the temptation to try a short cut, he came to realize by and by that, in confronting patients with personality disorders, the therapist must put his own person on the line. During his Freudian period, he saw psychoanalysis as the method of choice for bringing about this two-person engagement. After his break with the Viennese master, Jung began to denigrate Freudian therapy as mechanistic tinkering with psychic *apparatus,* and set himself the more ambitious task of the *cure of souls.* Before long he seemed to be offering, with his psychology of individuation, a method of redemption. More precisely, he seemed bent on obliterating the distinction between medical and spiritual concerns.

5

AN INEXORABLE MARRIAGE

Jung's lifelong hero complex had its seamy side. When, inevitably, his chosen idol proved a mere mortal, Jung would feel betrayed. His adoration turned to hatred, he would now debase with fierce sarcasm the icon he had revered. Late in 1902, when Bleuler's luster began to dim, and the "frosty fuddy-duddy" became visible behind the myth of the all-knowing chief, Jung found a new fetish: Pierre Janet, then France's foremost psychologist. Anxious to meet the new object of his worship in the flesh, Jung took a leave of absence from the Burghölzli. He was going to attend Janet's lectures at the Collège de France.

Like Bleuler and Freud, Janet failed to live up to the heroic role for which he had been cast. Yet he was a man of considerable stature. A pioneer in the study of hypnosis, an astute investigator of the paranormal, he was noted for his papers on Leonie, a girl with multiple selves. (This case was a model for Jung's study of the medium Helene P.) He was equally noted for his masterful clinical dissection of obsessives with their sterile pseudologic and their "execrable metaphysics."

Janet was a metaphysician of sorts himself. In the best and the worst French tradition, he had been drenched with the spirit of Cartesian analysis. Intensely religious in his youth, he strove in his manhood to reconcile religion, philosophy, and psychology—a pursuit haunting Jung. More lucid, and less of a visionary than Jung, Janet realized the formidable difficulty of this task. Unlike Jung, he had disciplined his mystical appetites and refused to leap to conclusions about the metaphysical import of paranormal events. He admitted that he had failed to realize his "marvelous" dream of a great philosophical synthesis; nevertheless, he "remained a philosopher."

As a psychologist, Janet was preoccupied (as was Jung) with the "economics" of psychic energy. His notions were rather simplistic. He believed that the human being is endowed at birth with a fixed psychic capital, different for each person—a sort of psychological trust fund. Some are born psychic millionaires; their energy being practically boundless, they can lavish it without counting. But for psychic paupers, matters are very different; even modest efforts can bankrupt them psychically and lead to states of depression and mental illness. To prevent or cure such illness it is necessary to curtail the *energy budget* of the psychically poor. Janet wrote that as yet "we know nothing of the nature of this psychic energy, but we must study its effects and succeed in measuring it, as the physicist measures an electric current without really comprehending its nature."

Jung was much taken with Janet's energetics of the psyche. A term frequently recurring in his writings is Janet's *abaissement du niveau mental* (lowering of the level of psychic energy) —a metaphor used by both men to "explain" dissociation and other symptoms of mental illness. Also Jung preferred by far Janet's neutral psychic energy to Freud's pansexual libido. But however attractive many of his ideas, as a person the genteel little Frenchman disappointed Jung. He failed to live up to the latter's notions of heroic stature. Besides, Janet showed little personal interest in the rather uncouth young Swiss psychiatrist with his guttural French. Extremely sensitive to any real or imagined slight, Jung felt rebuffed. He took his revenge by deriding Janet as a "hollow *causeur*," "a mere intellect, devoid of personality," "a typical mediocre bourgeois." Years later, in a letter to Freud, Jung called Janet "a vain old duffer, reeking of sterility." Jung based these epithets on Janet's refusal to eat from the Freudian tree of knowledge. Still later, when Jung's friendship with the Viennese master had wilted in its turn, he reinstated Janet as a great explorer of the unconscious—at the expense of papa Freud.

If in the winter of 1902–03 Janet disappointed Jung, Paris did not. Too poor to intoxicate himself on the luxuriant *Fleurs du Mal* celebrated by Baudelaire, too unconnected to be invited to the aristocratic salons where Janet was lionized, Jung got high on cheap Bordeaux and on the "petites sensations" flowing from Cezanne's mysterious paintings. He felt in an odd mood, "giddy and vulnerable." Also he was in love, and about to be married.

To know how Jung first caught sight of and, on the spot, "recognized" his future wife is to know Jung at his most authentic. It was an instant enchantment, fateful, preordained, inevitable: the stuff of legend. Jung met Emma for the first time during a holiday when, a young medical student, he visited friends of his family. As he entered the foyer of their elegant villa, he saw a young girl with braids, nymphlike, standing on the stairs. A brief glance—and Jung felt "deeply affected." He later said that he knew "immediately with absolute certainty that she would become my wife." A friend of Jung who accompanied him ridiculed this instant crush for the pubescent schoolgirl. And in fact, Jung's preordained love for Emma Rauschenbach was more tentative and intermittent than suited the myth he later spun around it. After his first meeting with Emma, Jung fell in love with other girls who, at the time, appeared similarly providential. But these affairs came to nothing, and six years after their fleeting encounter on the stairway, Jung formally wooed Emma Rauschenbach.

When Jung asked to marry her, he was turned down. A bitter memory was resurrected of his grandfather's rejection by Sophie Frey, the mayor's daughter. Had he overreached himself? Was he meant to repeat his grandfather's fate? Carl was less impulsive, and less versatile, than the elder Jung; unlike his grandfather, he had no ready replacement at hand whom he could marry on the spot. While still smarting over his defeat, he learned that his situation was less hopeless than he had surmised. He had been refused because Emma considered herself "engaged" to a young man whom she had kissed a few times. Her resolute mother, who had been smitten with the Reverend Paul Jung (Carl's father), was on Carl's side. She got Emma to dissolve the phantom engagement and then wrote Carl about this turn of events. Thus, in February 1903, they were married, Carl twenty-seven years old, Emma twenty.

Emma Rauschenbach was an heiress, the older of two daughters of a wealthy manufacturer. As a child, she was serious and shy, a loner (as Carl had been) who played by herself.

There was something Cassandra-like about her, a premonition of future disasters. When she was twelve, disaster hit the family: her father, an active, energetic man, went blind. Bitterness about his new dependency transformed him into a petulant tyrant. Emma, soft and vulnerable, had to bear the brunt of his resentment. She found her social life stifled; she was not allowed to go to college. By the time Carl appeared on the scene, she felt like a bird in a gilded cage, starving for excitement and intellectual food. Carl, oddly eloquent, overflowing with bold ideas, provided both. Her timidity made him expansive. He played the seasoned man of the world, the somber Othello to her innocent Desdemona, fascinating her with his put-on swagger and gauche charm.

Emma's childhood shyness followed her into married life. To the friends of the new couple, she appeared to be less complex, and less touchy, than her very sensitive husband who had acquired the nickname "The Prince on the Pea." She also appeared to be rather clinging; to those who knew Carl's impatient temperament, it seemed only a question of time till he would get tired of her. But in this respect appearances were deceptive. A photograph taken shortly before their wedding seems to support the thesis of her pliant dependency on Carl: the pair stand so close as to look like Siamese twins. Their inner arms are hidden from sight, and Emma appears to nestle against her sturdy fiancé. But a closer look shows that it is actually Carl who leans, at a barely perceptible angle, toward his bride; she stands straight and self-contained. This optical illusion, this gap between social appearance and psychological reality, became more pronounced with the years, became, in fact, the secret that cemented the relationship of Carl and Emma Jung.

The first years of their marriage were reasonably happy.

C. G. Jung—The Haunted Prophet

They first lived in a large apartment in the Burghölzli and then (from 1909 on) in the spacious villa that Carl built in Küsnacht, at the edge of the lake—with Emma's money. Gradually, he adopted a more lavish life-style, until his household included three servants: two maids and a gardener-factotum who also came to serve as chauffeur. His new-found wealth enabled Carl to indulge in his more expensive hobbies, in sailing, globe-trotting, and the collecting of rare books and objets d'art. But the fact that he was rich now did not resolve his "money complex" which continued to play a large role in his life. (Incidentally, money is a topic not much discussed in Jungian psychotherapy.) When Freud reproved him for his "taste for money-making" manifest in his "American dealings," Jung replied that he needed to make much money in order to "rid myself of the thought that I am nonviable." He added: "These are all frightful stupidities which can only be overcome by acting them out. . . ."

While Carl was acting out his money and power fantasies, Emma, with her zeal to learn, naturally fell into the role of his follower and student. She read every word he wrote as if it were Holy Writ and proved herself a devout Jungian. While bringing up the five children who were born at fairly regular intervals, she also managed to study mathematics—because "it teaches one to think"—Latin, and Greek. Despite her earnest attempts at mental acrobatics, she could hardly keep up with her exacting husband. Carl easily became impatient with the plodding slowness of her intellect, but he needed her as a sounding board. He required the echo of intuitive understanding that he took to be a feminine trait.

By and by, the romance of being the wife of the brilliant Carl Jung wore thin. Emma felt confined and began to chafe under her double role of wife-mother and student-child. Her sense of confinement grew when Carl insisted that he ought to analyze her. It was not her nature to complain, but a morose strain of her character, banished since she had left the paternal house, began to resurface. She found little solace in their social life which revolved around Carl, solely: women seemed to be fascinated by him and men to utterly ignore her. Reduced to being an onlooker in her own drawing room, she added to her sense of humiliation by "talking extra stupid in company."

For a long time, Carl remained blind to his wife's growing distress. He romanticized the early years of their life together. He believed that Emma was "bearing up splendidly" under his analysis. But gradually his rosy view of his marriage, and of marriage in general, changed, until he came to see it as "a brutal reality." Even so he regarded it as the crucial experiment and experience of the individual's life. When a colleague wrote to him that self-realization was possible without marriage, that self-analysis and meditation were sufficient, the middle-aged Jung demurred. He insisted that for the real self to emerge "a responsible relationship of some kind" is needed; for most people, this means marriage.

In his late forties Jung wrote a forceful essay on the psychology of marriage that clearly reflected the evolution of his own marriage. In this essay Jung sketched what he took to be a paradigm of the history of a typical marriage. Such a marriage, in Jung's view, usually comes about for reasons that are not what they seem to be. Young people believe that they "choose" a marriage partner and that this choice is freely made. In this they are mistaken. More often than not their choice is dictated by factors that elude them, i.e., by the unconscious. These unconscious factors loom large in "love at first sight." (The reader may remember that it was an instant crush sealed with a fleeting glance that led to Carl's union with Emma.)

The first phase of most marriages, according to Jung, is a stage of fantasied identity. It is a happy, but fragile stage. The seeming identity is based on the shared delusion that the partners are more similar (or complementary) than they really are. Sooner or later, this delusion will shatter under the impact of reality; while it lasts, though, those under its spell are blessed with a great richness of experience, often seen as a direct disclosure of the Divine. The transcendent force of this experience "obliterates and consumes everything individual. . . . The individual will, clinging to itself, is broken: the woman becomes mother, the man, father, and thus both are robbed of their freedom and are made instruments of the life force."

This extinction of individuality is temporary. After awhile, the submerged ego reasserts itself, smashing the fantasy of mutual identity. Then the stage is set for the unavoidable marital crisis (occurring usually during middle life) which actualizes previously latent conflicts. The ensuing turmoil leads either to a new, more stable equilibrium, based on conscious affirmation of oneself and the other, or it spells the end of the marriage.

It is clear that Jung's picture of the first happy phase of marriage describes the first years of *his* marriage. His analysis of the marital crisis of middle age is couched in terms that fit his and Emma's personalities—or, more exactly, his perception of them. Jung states that the "spiritual maturity" of each combatant is a crucial factor in their struggle. By spiritual maturity he means "a certain complexity of mind and nature." Trying to be objective, he writes that such complexity is not necessarily a very desirable trait; but his description of one partner as a "many-faceted gem" and of the other as a "simple cube" leaves little doubt about his private appraisal.

The many-faceted partner, Jung states, fascinates the simple one by offering a wide "array of possible experiences which leave little space for an independent life." To depict this interplay, Jung uses the analogy of the "container" and the "contained one." The latter has the easier role. She (to use the gender which Jung avoids using but to which he obviously refers) is too taken up with the marriage to look beyond its confines. Content in her containment, she is undivided in her loyalty and thus relatively whole. Her vulnerable spot is her dependence on a partner who almost by definition is not entirely reliable.

Things are more difficult for the "container." The inner dynamics of the marriage push him beyond its confines. "The simpler nature works on the more complex one like a room that is too small, that does not allow him enough space." Yet the containing one also yearns to be contained—a need his partner cannot meet. Thwarted in this crucial desire, he comes to experience his partner's single-minded loyalty as cloying. Eventually, he will seek outside the marriage the completion he cannot find within it.

The containing one, Jung writes, must take upon himself, consciously and resolutely, the guilt and anguish resulting from his transgression. The resulting struggle, with himself and others, uncovers his latent inner split. This split can no longer be circumscribed; it can only "be healed by a more complete laceration." If he is ready to bear the pain of this ordeal, the containing one will find in the end the inner wholeness that eluded him earlier.

Jung's tortured language in his marriage essay shows that he was ill at ease and rationalizing. He wanted to describe the internal workings of the typical marriage. What he actually depicted was his own torn self which could not find fulfillment with a single partner. He required a kind of double marriage, and its inherent tensions; only in such a triangle did he find safety and the intermittent intimacy he needed. In his essay he succumbed to the psychologist's eternal temptation: he unwittingly codified the rules regulating his own conduct as universal laws of human behavior. He seems to have managed, at any rate, to impose his law upon Emma who came to accept the "brutal reality" of the Jungian marriage. She was rewarded by Carl's gratitude, and by being allowed to share in the gifts of his "many-faceted" nature.

It was part of the brutal reality of Jung's marriage that he had little time and feeling to spare for his family, either in his middle years or later. Like the Swiss saint "Brother Klaus" whom he admired, Carl led essentially a solitary life. Brother Klaus had built himself a hermit cell near the house he occupied with his family. To such a refuge, his self-built tower in Bollingen, Jung often repaired for long periods; and within this refuge, there was an inner sanctum, a room forbidden to all but Jung himself. His family, much of the time, was more of an abstract idea than a living reality for him. Even when he stayed in Küsnacht with them, he tended to be withdrawn and inaccessible. Exhausted from a hard day's work with his analytic foster children, he would often be silent and glum at the dinner table. If he did talk, he was likely to be caustic, mocking everyone—from his mother, who as long as she lived was the regular butt of his jokes at Sunday dinner, to his former chief Eugen Bleuler. One of his favorite anecdotes, trotted out regularly and gleefully at mealtime, was about a manic patient who had once jammed a chamber pot over Bleuler's head—a crown that Jung obviously found not unsuited for his former patron. As soon as the maid was summoned to remove the dessert dishes, he would retreat behind his newspaper or closet himself in his study.

Under this regime, his children came to feel like semi-orphans. This father, so remote, so quick to burst into rage, so ready to rail at everything, including God, seemed both shadowy and dangerous. One of his daughters, fearing his mocking disapproval, became afraid to say her bedtime prayers at night, and felt clumsily stupid under his cool, appraising gaze. Another daughter wondered whether he would even remember her name if the mother did not quickly prompt him. Emma Jung intervened often, soothing the children after a paternal tantrum, intimating that his thunderbolts were not lethal.

Jung tried to explain his aloofness from his children with the lame excuse that he did not wish to smother them with his powerful personality. He cited the fact that all of them married as proof of the correctness of his policy; to him, their later family life indicated that they did not suffer from excessive "father-complexes." That his offspring took no interest in his work and were not inclined to follow in his footsteps did not seem to trouble him.[1]

Toward Emma, Jung's attitude remained complex. In his typical fashion, he tried to master this complexity with the aid of a conceptual schema. But Jung's theory of the "container" and the "contained" was too naive. It would have required the subtlety of a Marcel Proust to capture the incessant shifts of focus, underground tremors, and searing paradoxes of mar-

[1]Years later, as adults, two of his daughters began to show an active interest in Jung's analytical psychology.

riage. A Proust would also have seen the impossibility of a general theory of marriage. Jung, lacking a finely tuned sense of psychological nuances, did not. He tried to lock people and their actions into crude conceptual boxes. The easily predictable result was that people and events constantly perplexed him by failing to live up to his rules. Jung's theory of marriage as a container tells us how he perceived his marriage in middle life. As a paradigm of marriage in general, and even as an objective appraisal of his own marriage, it is useless.

True, Carl was Emma's spiritual and intellectual guide; as such, he was able to offer her great riches and perhaps even a kind of spiritual "home ground." But in the realm of feeling, Emma was by far the richer personality. In this area, which provides the nourishing soil for *all* growth, Emma, embracing and supportive, provided Carl with a secure base. Her inherited wealth made her also the source of material security. Although he was loath to admit it, Carl needed her custodial presence. Whenever he was traveling, he would write her often and at great length. And throughout the marital storms unleashed by his affair with Toni Wolff, he never seriously questioned the permanence of his marriage.

The marriage survived in the end because Emma discreetly guarded its innermost secret: Carl could think and profess that he "contained" her, while he actually was—to use once more his cumbersome term—the contained one. Emma, benign and steady as his mother had never been, played her role flawlessly. Not once did she force Carl to confront the fact that he was her adopted sixth child. No wonder Emma in later life looked the very epitome of motherliness, a motherliness in full flower, the potential of which Carl may have dimly sensed on the stairway in Schaffhausen. If so, he never let on. Instead, masking his need, he adopted the stance of guru to the simple cube who was his mother-wife.

6

SIGMUND FREUD— A MUTUAL ENCHANTMENT

The Jung–Freud friendship was, in the main, epistolary. It was prepared, initiated, sustained, amplified, and eventually destroyed, through letters. Face-to-face meetings between the two men were few, brief (except for their 1909 trip to the U.S.), and far between—mere interludes in their correspondence.

The first move was made by Jung. Early in 1906 he sent his book on word association to Freud. In a short but cordial note of thanks, Freud treated Jung's work as proof that "everything I have said about the hitherto unexplored fields of our theory is true." He felt confident, he wrote, that Jung would still often find occasion to back him up, but he also was ready to "gladly accept correction" if called for. As it turned out, Jung was naive or disingenuous enough to take Freud's invitation to refute him at face value.

After an interval of a few months, Freud sent a recently published work of his to Jung. In his reply, the latter voiced the hope that Freud's "scientific following" would continue to grow, without making quite clear whether he himself was part of this following. He did make clear, though, that he had just defended Freud in "a lively correspondence" against the attacks of a certain professor Aschaffenburg. Jung viewed Aschaffenburg's strictures as pitifully shallow, but intimated that he, too, had misgivings—presumably less shallow; he found it hard to follow Freud's notions of the sexual origin of hysteria. (Had he wanted to, Freud could have recognized even then, in this first bit of "correction," a man unsuited for apostleship.) Jung's letter concluded with the news that Professor Bleuler, his chief, had of late been "completely converted" to the cause of psychoanalysis. Whether this conversion was due to the merit of Freud's ideas or to Jung's proselytizing, Jung did not say. His whole letter was redolent with emotional ambiguity— as was most of the correspondence to follow.

Freud answered Jung's letter by return mail. He maintained this habit of replying on the spot throughout their exchange, thus putting the less prompt Jung into the uneasy position of being forever in arrears. In this letter, Freud was hopeful that Jung would eventually accept his sexual theories; Jung's recent "splendid" paper on a case of obsessional neurosis augured well in this respect. If Aschaffenburg, whom Jung had offered as a common enemy, opposed psychoanalysis, it was mainly because of his need to repress sexuality, "that troublesome factor so unwelcome in good society." Such repression, Freud indicated, is based on "inner resistance to the truth." Rather than waste time on Aschaffenburg's "inanities," he would save his energy for those able to "cast off the last vestiges of pusillanimity" in their thinking.

Freud's derogatory tone toward his critics struck a responsive chord in Jung, who was to lash out promptly at the "inanities" of another opponent, a Professor Hoche. These diatribes against colleagues escalated quickly. In strident tones Jung spoke of "psychopaths" and of "pachyderms" that "cannot understand anything unless you write it out as big as your fist on their hide"; he hurled epithets such as "vain old duffer," "totally impotent gasbag," "confounded fusspot," "incredibly plebeian," "miserable pen-pusher," "damned swine," "complete nut," "slimy bastard," etc. Freud, more subdued, could not quite keep up with this flood of invective, but his letters, too, teemed with "hidings" and "whippings" he wanted to administer to unbelievers.

But if Jung found it easy to echo, and amplify, Freud's disparagement of his critics, he confessed himself alarmed by the "positivism" (read: dogmatism) of Freud's presentation. He felt queasy about imputing any deviation from Freud's truth to "resistance." His own work, he pleaded, ought to be "tailored a bit" to his subjective standpoint, ought to maintain "the hint of an independent judgment." Afraid of displeasing Freud, he was quick to add that he viewed such a show of reserve as politic, as a clever stratagem, meant to make psychoanalysis more palatable to that "seven-headed monster," the academic public. While Freud questioned the efficacy of Jung's attempts at diplomacy, he seemed blind to their deeper psychological import. He failed to see that Jung's maneuvers were self-protective. Under the cover of making Freud's cause more salable, Jung was trying to defend his autonomy vis-à-vis

Freud. But this autonomy—as the need for such contrivances suggests—had already been forfeited.

Jung's conscience was uneasy about his equivocations. When a letter from Freud containing some criticism of a Jungian paper seemed to end rather abruptly, Jung was worried. Cautiously he inquired whether his calculated reticence had displeased Freud. The latter's reply, soothing while not completely reassuring, was a masterpiece of indirectness: Jung need not fret; Freud is enthusiastic about Jung's work; the very fact that he offers criticism ought to put Jung's mind at rest; if Freud had disliked the work, he—the nondiplomat—would have summoned enough diplomacy to hide his misgivings; it would be unwise to offend such an able helper, etc.

Thus the first few letters, with their subtle thrusts and parries, pointed already to the underlying tensions which later, inexorably, would destroy the bond between the two men. Despite the signs of latent conflict, the two main protagonists —as is customary in such situations—hoodwinked themselves about the real goings-on: their blindness was the more piquant by virtue of their eminence as code-breakers of the human mind.

Freud was blind to his own possessiveness, to the coercive nature of his love, the rigidity of his dogmatism, and his masochistic lapses that taunted Jung beyond endurance. And Jung, caught in the web of his ambivalence, falling into the coveted and onerous role of favorite son, was oblivious, for too long, of his acts of self-betrayal, of the baseness of his dissembling, and of the smoldering rage within. His brutal outbursts, in his last letters to Freud, were due to his belated sense of shame at having danced, for six long years, to Freud's compelling and— in Jung's hindsight—insidious tune.

But in the winter of 1906, when the correspondence between the two men began to intensify, Jung was far from sensing its denouement (and so was Freud). By December of that year, he was already deploring his lack of personal contact with Freud as a "regrettable defect" in his training. Freud, eagerly picking up the hint, extended a semi-invitation. Perhaps Jung, who had earlier written about his wish to see America, would come first to Vienna, which was, after all, nearer? This cue was sufficient for Jung. He declared his intention to visit Vienna in April (1907), during his spring vacation. In his reply, Freud said he was delighted that their meeting would take place during Easter when he himself had a few days off. Whereupon Jung changed his plans, moving the date of his trip ahead to early March. Freud asked that in this case Jung should arrange to have a Sunday available, his weekdays being filled to the brim "with the occupations known to you."

Despite these maneuvers, the meeting between the two men materialized on Sunday, March 3, 1907. Jung was accompanied by Emma and an assistant, Ludwig Binswanger. The first impressions were favorable. Freud's simple charm was as obvious as his delight at meeting Jung and his retinue. Impatient with small talk, he at once asked the two men about their dreams. Jung obliged with a dream which, in Freud's view, pointed to usurpation fantasies. However Freud did not take umbrage at these fantasies. In fact, he very soon was referring to Jung as his "scientific heir." In no time at all, both men were visibly under the spell of a mutual enchantment. The constellation was favorable: Jung had come to pay homage to Freud's genius that had lighted up the dark shafts of the unconscious; Freud, shunned by most medical men, was moved by this recognition from the gifted Swiss psychiatrist. Both men wanted much more than a mere exchange of ideas; both, though "happily married," felt lonely and were yearning for a providential other. The gap left in Freud's life by the break with Wilhelm Fliess had remained unfilled. Among the motley crew of his Viennese followers, no one was close to him nor his intellectual equal. Freud was aching for a spiritual heir in whose very being he could delight. (Little did he suspect at the time that he was going to find this heir, in the end, in one of his daughters.)

Jung, for his part, had been searching all along for the spiritual mentor his own father had failed to be. This quest was the more passionate for being mostly unconscious. Bleuler and Janet had not fitted the heroic father mold. But things promised to be quite different with Freud. Here was a man of visible genius, imposing yet modest, a stranger to triteness, radiating spiritual power. To Jung it must have seemed the fulfillment of a lifelong dream that this great man talked to him for hours, listened intently to his torrent of speech, and obviously rejoiced in his rich fantasy and sheer energy. But the realization of this dream must also have stirred up dark undercurrents. To be anointed the spiritual son of the mighty Viennese prophet might lead to a great destiny, but it was also bound to inflame Jung's deep ambivalence, his oscillation between revolt and surrender, in the face of authority. Yet if he was aware of danger signals, Jung chose to ignore them. He was too exhilarated at having found, at last, the embodiment of his hero.

Freud was equally oblivious. Older and more settled than Jung, he was less ambivalent. His delight with this high-spirited follower come to him from Zurich was boundless. Even Jung's intellectual pretenses, his occasional slights of Freud's hard-won knowledge, did not dampen Freud's enthusiasm. For once mellow, Freud misjudged the extent of Jung's ambiguity. But, then, neither of the two men was, in his daily life, a very shrewd judge of people.

Thus from the very first, their differences were played down and intellectualized. As he had done in his letters, Jung expressed some misgivings about theoretical issues. His point of attack was always the same: Freud seemed to put too much emphasis on sexuality; in particular, his attempt to derive spiritual life from repressed sexual urges was problematical. Only much later did Jung recognize the personal antagonism hidden behind his "theoretical" arguments; in his typology he asserted that his clash with Freud arose from the ineluctable fatalities of inborn character, from their deepest, prerational commitments, and hence was unresolvable.

But initially, in the face of their growing friendship, their differences seemed minor. Both were elated by their first meeting. At the end of March—three and a half weeks after leaving Vienna—Jung wrote a long letter to Freud. He apologized for his prolonged "reaction time," explaining that he had wanted to deal first with the "complexes" stirred up by his visit. Jung reported that Bleuler's resistances to psychoanalysis "are more vigorous than ever." But he himself is no longer beset by doubts about the truth of Freud's theories. The last shreds of disbelief have been dispelled by his stay in Vienna. Does he dare hope for a return visit by Freud to Zurich? Such an event would be "seventh heaven" for him.

In subsequent letters, Jung's pleading for more personal contact persisted; so did his near-religious tone: "Where so much remains still dark to us outsiders only faith can help." This faith is best promoted by knowing Freud "in the flesh." His personal knowledge of Freud, Jung wrote, has completely

"reformed" his thinking. The views he has held in the prerefor-
mation period, a time that seems already very distant (though
actually only a few weeks have passed since his conversion),
appear to him now not only "intellectually defective," but also
"morally inferior." Jung is even ready now to swallow the
difficult Freudian dogma that opposition to psychoanalysis is
caused by affects, "especially sexual affects." To know the
Freudian science, Jung proclaimed, is to have eaten from the
tree of paradise, is to have gained clairvoyance.

In October 1907, six months after their first meeting, Jung's
infatuation reached a climax. In a letter to Freud, he admitted
to "something like a religious crush" for him, adding that this
worship, with its erotic overtones, struck him as somehow
disgusting. Having suffered in boyhood a homosexual assault
from an older man he idolized, Jung was afraid, he said, of
getting too close to Freud. In his next letter, he retreated a bit,
mentioning a dream in which Freud appeared to him as a "very
very frail old man." Only a few days later he analyzed his
worship of Freud rather coolly as a compensation of his "earlier
very vivid religiosity." A process of objectification had begun;
this development may have been not unwelcome to Freud.

Early in 1908 Freud made a "well-prepared" advance,
changing from a more formal mode of address to a simple "dear
friend." Jung replied that this "undeserved gift" was a high
point of his life. He begged Freud to let him enjoy his friendship "not as one between equals but as that of father and son."
This humility masked a need for distance. Jung continued to
address Freud with the rather punctilious "Lieber Herr Professor."

During the prime of their friendship, Jung organized the
first International Congress of Psychoanalysis (Salzburg, April

1908). He insisted on naming it "The Conference for Freudian Psychology," although others would have preferred a more neutral label. But Jung's hero cult was not to be denied. This cult had a very militant side. Thus, in a letter of that period, Jung exulted that a forthcoming book on hysteria would tear "a bomb-size crater" in the ranks of Freud's German opponents.

The Salzburg Congress of 1908 was attended by forty-two participants. Besides the large Viennese contingent and the six Swiss headed by Bleuler and Jung, there were five Germans (among them, Karl Abraham), two Hungarians, two Englishmen, and one lone American (A. A. Brill). Papers were read, and it was decided to found a psychoanalytic yearbook, to be edited by Jung. Freud's infatuation with the Swiss latecomer did not exactly endear Jung to the old guard of Viennese analysts; and now Jung was to be the final judge of papers submitted to their new journal; it was almost more than the Austrians could stomach.

Among the participants at the Salzburg Congress was the gifted but eccentric Graz psychiatrist, Otto Gross. At Freud's urging, Gross, an opium and cocaine addict, committed himself to Burghölzli where Jung was to psychoanalyze him. Jung diagnosed him as a case of obsessional neurosis and decided not to interfere, initially, with his drug habit. He did not want to "upset the analysis by arousing feelings of privation."

The analysis made very rapid progress at first. It was unusual in that mutuality prevailed: whenever Jung got stuck with his analysis of Gross, Gross analyzed *him.* Jung felt that his own psychic health benefited from this procedure. But the main beneficiary of this experiment, in Jung's eyes, was Gross. After only two weeks, Jung wrote Freud that he had successfully concluded the treatment: Gross was now voluntarily going through with opium withdrawal. Only the mopping-up of a few secondary obsessions remained. In his reply, Freud expressed amazement about the speed of the cure; he himself would have needed much longer to arrive at such a result.

Freud's skepticism—if such it was—was well-founded. Three weeks later the mopping-up operation was still not completed; on the contrary, it was encompassing more and more territory, undoing the apparent miracle cure. Gross's case proving unexpectedly intractable, Jung changed his diagnosis from obsessional neurosis to schizophrenia. He decided to undertake an experiment never tried before; to cure a case of acute schizophrenia by means of psychoanalysis. Jung worked terribly hard. He held marathon sessions with Gross; one of these lasted twenty-four hours until both were completely exhausted and could no longer keep their eyes open. But Gross defeated the heroic efforts of his caretaker by climbing over a garden wall and escaping. The next day he sent Jung a note asking for money to pay his hotel bill.

Jung took this failure hard. He had taken a liking to, and obviously identified with, Gross, considering him a sort of twin brother "but for the dementia praecox." After Gross's flight, Jung saw him as doomed. He felt that Gross had no inkling of the revenge that reality, ignored by him, was going to wreak. In Jung's eyes, Gross had become, by then, a man whom "life is *bound* to reject." This time, Jung's prognosis was accurate. An anarchist and apostle of orgiastic sexuality, Gross managed for a while to gather a group of admirers around him, but after a wretched life, spent in the shadow of unshakable drug addiction, he died at forty-two under somewhat mysterious circumstances; it was either direct or indirect suicide.

Two years later, Jung was to undertake another attempt to save a colleague staggering at the edge of madness, Johann Honegger. This attempt also ended tragically, with Honegger's suicide.

During the period 1908 to 1909, Freud became gradually addicted to Jung's letters. He felt "impoverished" when their correspondence flagged. Stung by Jung's silences, he would urgently plead for a sign of life—once or twice even by telegram. Jung's letters, on the other hand, had by then become less worshipful; they had also grown more apologetic. In endless variations, Jung taxed himself for being a lazy correspondent. But repeatedly he would let several days pass before concluding a letter—unusual for him.

Jung's apologetic tone intensified after a brief visit to Vienna (March 1909) during which he had startled Freud by interpreting a few cracking sounds in a bookcase as paranormal manifestations. On his return to Zurich he expressed concern that Freud might have been put off by his "spookery." An enigmatic parenthesis alluded to Wilhelm Fliess, Freud's former friend, and "insanity." But he also wrote of a "madly interesting" patient who had produced "first-rate spiritualistic" phenomena, "though so far only once in my presence." This patient, he added, had given him a curious feeling that underneath her personal complexes there must be a universal one, "having to do with the prospective tendencies in man." He cited his wife on whom this case has made "the deepest impression." The whole letter sounded rather flighty, as Jung himself noted. His oversensitive antennae had picked up what he took to be signs of distrust from Freud.

In the meantime, Freud was mulling over a matter that caused him almost as much concern as Jung's obsession with poltergeists. He had been invited by an American college, Clark University, to participate in celebrating its twentieth anniversary. Despite the flattering tone of the invitation (which stated that Freud's attendance would give American psychotherapy "a mighty impetus"), he at first declined; the timing (July 1909) seemed bad and the travel allowance of $400 insufficient. He did not feel rich enough "to spend five times that much to give Americans an impetus." Jung argued that Freud's going to America would mean good publicity for their cause; it might even bring money. Freud was apt to earn his travel expenses many times over by attracting rich American patients—as had happened to Janet. Wealthy Americans, according to Jung, paid fabulous fees; recently a German psychiatrist had raked in 50,000 marks for a single consultation in California.

Freud's doubts dissolved when Clark University postponed its celebration to September and almost doubled his travel allowance. In fact, having decided to make the trip and having persuaded his disciple Sandor Ferenczi to accompany him, Freud felt quite excited about his American venture. His enthusiasm took a quantum leap when in late spring Jung was also invited to Clark. Jung immediately took a cabin on the S. S. *George Washington*—"unfortunately only a very expensive one was left," he reported to Freud—on which Freud and Ferenczi had booked passage. Freud's jubilant response made clear to Jung how much his presence meant to Freud.

During the nine-day journey from Bremen to New York, Jung and Freud spent much time analyzing each other's dreams. Jung thought that this exchange benefited Freud greatly; at the same time he felt that his own dreams were not dealt with very well by Freud. The latter seemed at a loss in the face of dreams that churned up material from the deepest layers of the unconscious—dreams of which Jung had aplenty. To one of these dreams in particular, Jung attached great significance. It was a typical Jungian dream, with vast underground vaults dating from prehistoric antiquity. On the floor of one vault, thickly covered with dust, Jung found two very old, half-decayed human skulls.

When Freud was told this dream, he focused almost exclusively on the two skulls. Again and again he asked Jung to whom they belonged. This insistence angered Jung, who knew what Freud was driving at: Jung was to admit to secret death wishes toward people close to him. Certain that he was free of such sinister impulses, Jung finally allowed that the skulls were those of his wife and his sister-in-law. In doing so, he thought he was lying. The extorted "confession" left him with a bitter taste. But he was afraid of displeasing Freud by insisting on his own point of view. Thus he contrived to say "something that suited his [Freud's] theories."

This charade was not without irony. Here, analyzing each other, were the two great founders of modern depth psychology. They had often stated that the analyst must be absolutely truthful, without illusions about himself, and proof against the temptation to violate others. And yet, interpreting each other's dreams, with the vast expanse of the ocean as backdrop, they broke their most basic maxims. Jung's naivete was as extreme as Freud's doctrinaire impatience. Believing that his complex dream had only one "true" meaning, Jung was blind to his own ambivalences. Unwittingly, he confessed the unconscious truth in the guise of a conscious lie. Freud, on his part, was too dogmatic, too sure of the absolute validity of *his* truth. He left little room for the younger man to find his own way, perhaps apprehensive about the direction it might take.

Such apprehension would not have been amiss. For Jung,

the dream in question was a "Big Dream." Its imagery seemed to summon him to plunge beneath his personal prehistory to those deepest psychic layers where the individual's fate merges with the impersonal river of human history. These first musings about what Jung later called the "collective unconscious" were soon to lead far afield from Freudian psychology.

At the time, Jung concealed his growing estrangement from Freud. So, when they landed in New York on August 30, a cordial understanding appeared to prevail between them. Jung was much taken with the miracles of American technology, but he was also acutely aware of the human sacrifices with which this progress had been bought. The hectic bustle of New York did not agree with him, nor did American food. He decided to fast. Feeling weary and out of sorts, he dragged himself to the Museum of Natural History where the sight of the ancient monsters in the palaeontological section—"the creation-nightmares of God"—fascinated him.

Much more to Jung's taste than New York was New England with its woods and lakes, its idyllic towns, brightly painted houses and well-tended lawns. He noted the signs of prosperity that abounded everywhere. Like many Europeans before and after him, Jung was amazed by the openness of the American life-style, the rareness of garden walls and fences, the large windows exposing the interior of private homes, the open doors of houses and rooms, including bathrooms. This goldfish-bowl existence, reflected also in the gossip columns of newspapers, felt rather strange to Jung. But he also recognized immediately how much the starched rectitude of New England's puritan upper class resembled the "scary respectability" of Swiss patricians.

Jung's lectures at Clark University, like Freud's, were tailored to the presumed American mentality. Jung was as down-to-earth as he was capable of being. He talked mainly about his work with the Word Association Test, stressing its uses as a tool of criminology. Despite superficial affinities, he experienced the American mentality as alien. His own outlook and his intellectual premises were manifestly different from those of the Americans he met. He felt that if his or Freud's ideas were ever going to be adopted in America, they would be radically transformed in the process, perhaps beyond recognition. Jung subsequently puzzled for years over the riddle of the American mind, more enigmatic to him than the mentality of the Chinese.

However, there was one eminent American he met in Worcester with whom he felt an immediate kinship: William James. The two men shared, first of all, a deep contempt for most academic psychology with its excruciating pedantry. James once remarked bitingly of the "functional" psychology of Professor Edward Titchener, then in vogue at American universities, that its main *function* was to secure the survival of as many psychology professors as possible. Jung endorsed such sentiments with enthusiasm. In addition, both men shared a strong interest in philosophy and parapsychology. They talked much about James's experiments with the medium Eleonore Piper, who maintained that she was in touch with the spirits of the dead. Jung was enchanted by James's open-mindedness and simple directness, his urbane ease and encyclopedic knowledge. He was chagrined to learn from some hints that James was not taken quite seriously by Professor Stanley Hall, who hosted Freud and Jung during their stay in Worcester. Hence his delight when he saw James repaying Hall's condescension with a witty gesture. Arriving at Hall's house to participate in a colloquium, he greeted his host with "I've brought some papers which may interest you"—and then, instead of the expected documents, whipped out a bundle of dollar bills. James apologized profusely for his "faux pas" and produced the proper papers. But those present knew Hall as a relentless fund raiser and wondered whether James's error had been unintentional in the least.

In his letters home, Jung complained about the hectic pace of the Clark festivities and about the "mummery" of academic solemnity in which he found himself immersed. But he obviously enjoyed being lionized by his American hosts, and he thought the American audiences who seemed to soak up his words very likable indeed. He could not resist writing his wife how, during a garden party, he had been the center of a "court" of five women and had even managed to get off a few jokes in (rather poor) English. Unfamiliar with the relish of American reporters for personal interviews, and thus overestimating the importance of being written up in a newspaper, he noted after an interview with a Boston journalist: "We are the men of the hour here. It feels very good to be able to live out this side of things for once. I feel that my libido is enjoying it enormously. . . ." It is understandable that Jung and Freud, ostracized by much of the scientific community in Europe, made the most of the homage paid to them in America. When Freud was awarded his honorary degree, he declared that this event seemed to him like the realization of a long-standing dream. Jung's feelings, in this instance, paralleled those of Freud.

Before returning home, Jung, Freud, and Ferenczi spent a few days, with forty other guests, in the Adirondacks at the camp of the Harvard neurologist James Putnam. Jung was much taken with the area's wild, glacial scenery of field, lake, and Ice Age forest. But by the time he reembarked in New York (September 21), he felt exhausted. He declared that he found it easy to shake the dust of America from his boots. Yet in contrast to Freud, who diagnosed the bold American experiment as a "gigantic mistake," Jung appraised the United States as a "wonderland" in which an ideal way of life had become a reality. He maintained that American men were extremely well off, but noted that the position of American women, even if they were ensconced on pedestals, was highly problematical. He saw American civilization as anticipating the future social trends of European countries and recognized the havoc wrought in the minds of Americans by the unresolved dilemmas of the Negro question. But the overall impression he gained on his trip to the New World was positive. Jung therefore seized an early opportunity for another visit, whereas Freud never again set foot on what was to him the very alien soil of America.

7

THE BREAK
WITH FREUD

Shortly after his return from the United States, Jung had a new letterhead printed sporting his American "LL.D." If the trip to Worcester had enhanced his self-esteem, it had also cooled his admiration for Freud. Yet he found it necessary to maintain the stance of the worshipful follower. So adept was he that Freud, an unseeing King Lear, saw fit to bestow upon him larger and larger tracts of his realm. It would be three more years before Jung's disaffection finally worked its way to the surface.

First, though, Jung had to topple another master: Eugen Bleuler. Chafing under the authority of this amiably pallid man, Jung became by turns sullen and provocative. When Bleuler refused to be provoked, Jung forced the issue by leaving the Burghölzli in the fall of 1909. He said that he felt over-worked, but he clearly meant to shake off the less consequential of his two mentors. After the break, Jung felt more upset than he had expected. Once again, he confided to Freud, he had underestimated the intensity of his father complex.

As for Freud, he continued to display a rapt benevolence toward Jung. This emboldened Jung to propose that psycho-analysis become the catalyst of a new ecstatic religiosity, trans-forming "Christ back in the soothsaying god of the vine, which he was." No less was needed, Jung held, than to "absorb the . . . instinctual forces of Christianity for the *one* purpose of making the cult and the sacred myth what they once were—a drunken feast of joy where man regained the ethos and holiness of an animal." However bewildered Freud may have been by his disciple's Dionysian ramblings, his reply was mild, with only the slightest hint of ironic reproof. "Yes, in you the tempest rages," he noted, disavowing any intent to found a new religion. Altogether, he showed more concern for Jung's remissness as a correspondent than for his verbal, and mental, excesses.

The following spring, at the congress of Freudians in Nuremberg, Freud insisted that Jung be elected president of the newly founded International Psychoanalytic Association. In the process, he had to overcome a palace revolt of his Viennese followers, who had been suspicious of Jung ever since he joined their movement. They saw him as an opportunistic power-grabber, puffed up with haughty arrogance; of late, they had added to their list of grievances the dark suspicion that the "blond Siegfried," as they came to call Jung, was something of an antisemite. And now the old man wanted to make this braggart, to whom he had taken such a doting fancy, the head of their society, with dictatorial powers. It was almost more than they could bear. Freud had to make a melodramatic last-minute appeal to the Viennese faction to overcome their objections to Jung. His passion, more than his reasons, prevailed. Jung was elected as president of the new society, despite the tooth-gnashing opposition of a few Viennese hold-outs.

The situation was paradoxical in that Jung himself was a rather reluctant leader of the Freudian host. He was too self-willed and impatient, too devoid of diplomatic tact, to wholly enjoy his new administrative chores. Also, his sensitive egotism made him quickly realize that the honors heaped upon him meant that he was to nurse and promote the brainchild of another man—a man, moreover, whose authority was tarnished in his eyes. It was a false position, bound to become more onerous with time. Its falseness led Jung to overprotest his filial piety. Exasperated by Freud's habit of taking these protestations at face value, he was driven, in the end, to use brutality to free himself from the cloying Freudian meshes.

The potent blend of despotism and masochism that Jung found so irritating in Freud he was to display himself toward a protégé of his own, the psychiatrist Johann Honegger. Then an intern at the Burghölzli, Honegger was a radiant young man, keen and subtle-minded, a witty debater with an easy charm and a cheerful intensity that greatly appealed to Jung. That this radiance had a darker aspect was revealed to Jung when Honegger consulted him about a loss of his sense of reality that had lasted for several days. The lapse was diagnosed by Jung as neurotic. He advised Honegger to set out on a course of self-analysis.

In actuality, this luminous young man, fated to embody the myth of the sacrificial hero with which Jung was then preoccupied, was nearer psychosis than Jung realized at the time. Like many borderline psychotics, Honegger had an uncanny knack for reading the unconscious of others. He helped Jung shed light on some of his more obscure, elusive dreams. Gradually, their frequent contacts developed into an informal analysis which—as with Otto Gross—was to some degree mutual. Honegger's gracious integrity was much to Jung's liking. He is "honest to the core, considerably more honest than I, I'd say," Jung wrote to Freud, hinting that Honegger was becoming *his* disciple—Jung's Jung, as it were.

This discipleship, calculated to make Freud jealous, was not without its own problems. Jung hinted that he wanted Honegger to assist him in his private practice but could not quite bring himself to make a definite offer, partly because of the expense involved. Yet when Honegger, tired of waiting, joined the staff of a clinic near Montreux, Jung was painfully stung. "Now my libido is thrashing around for a suitable object," he lamented to Freud. Unable to find a "suitable" substitute, he invited Honegger to return to Zurich, but imposed a condition: Honegger ought to finish his medical dissertation before joining him. He also let it be known that Honegger ought to work harder, to become less self-indulgent and less addicted to Jung's approval. Freud, informed of these dealings, cautioned Jung to be less stern with Honegger. Not everybody, Freud noted, was fit to emulate Jung's "independence in his work habits from human libido"; Honegger was made of softer stuff and could not be cast into an exact Jungian mold. It was better to take him as he was, shaping him on the basis of his own nature, rather than trying to force him into another's form.

Jung agreed in principle but was not capable of that degree of laissez-faire. As soon as Honegger returned, he was treated very visibly as the junior partner, berated for his lax work habits and his refusal to renounce "living by the pleasure principle." Feeling overworked himself, and getting less help from his assistant than he had hoped for, Jung failed to make allowances for Honegger's latent psychosis, was, perhaps, not even aware of it. Honegger's difficulties, Jung felt, were exacerbated by his troubled relationship with his fiancée Helene Widmer. He thought the couple mismatched and did not hide his feelings. Finding the situation "sickly and unendurable," he sent Freud Mephistophelean comments about Honegger's "mess." He apparently nudged his indecisive assistant to break with Helene and was pleased when the break was finally consummated. Jung opined that by disengaging himself, Honegger had probably saved his skin. A few months later, Honegger was dead. He had killed himself, at the age of twenty-five, with an injection of morphine. The break with his fiancée had been followed shortly by his rupture with Jung and by his joining the staff of the asylum Rheinau near Zurich.

At first, Jung seemed rather unmoved by Honegger's suicide. In a brief, laconic note informing Freud of the event, he harked back to the theme of Honegger's addiction to the pleasure principle; this tragic flaw was probably the ultimate cause of his early death. Freud agreed, but also voiced the melancholy thought that, perhaps, "we wear out quite a few men." Refusing to take his friend's stoicism at face value, Freud insisted that Honegger's death must have been a severe blow to Jung—which indeed it was. When the blow finally registered, Jung was beset by severe pangs of guilt. He began to think that his lack of therapeutic skill, his inadequate attempts to analyze Honegger's psychotic fantasies, had led to his death. "What if this view should be confirmed?" he wrote to Freud. "I have the feeling that, with intense inner resistance, I am practicing vivisection on human beings."

The tragic episode of Honegger's suicide, in March 1911, marked the beginning of Jung's open estrangement from Freud. His struggle with a "devilish" case of schizophrenia at that time led him to conclude that in such cases therapy ought to focus on bringing the psychotic's unconscious fantasies to light. Had he done so with Honegger, he might have saved him. When Freud questioned the value of this therapeutic strategy, voicing doubt that it could have cured Honegger, Jung rejoined with unaccustomed sharpness: "That it is *not* of great therapeutic importance to get patients to produce their latent fantasies seems to me a very dubious proposition."

This rejoinder heralded the onset of Jung's active struggle to emerge from Freud's shadow. He was then working on a book in which he advanced rather un-Freudian notions about the concept and the metamorphoses of the libido.[1] Afraid of incurring Freud's displeasure, he kept crucial parts of the "heretical" work under wraps for a long time, agonizing over its completion. To hatch this particular work, and thus openly to "compete with the hen," seemed to Jung a "risky business" for which he had to summon all his courage. Freud's manifestly dim view of the egg-hatching Alfred Adler was doing at the time was not likely to allay Jung's fears.

From early 1911 on, Jung's letters showed a gradual stiffening of opposition to Freud. Tentative though his initial acts of defiance might have been, they clearly stood out *as* defiance. Thus Freud had only to note in a letter that children's dreams were exempt from the complex symbolism typical of adult

[1] *Transformations and Symbols of the Libido*

dreams, for Jung to present him, by return mail, with his four-year-old daughter's dream of symbolic foreskin and glans. As soon as Freud suggested that Jung set too much stock by the latent fantasies of psychotics, which actually were akin to the cultivated daydreams of neurotics, Jung countered that these fantasies, slighted by Freud, "bring the outside to the inside as nothing else can." More tellingly, when Freud stigmatized Adler's defection as "a nice little piece of paranoia," Jung responded with an alarming ambiguity that left Freud sorely troubled.

The impending break, then, was prepared by two, closely linked, factors: Jung's intellectual departure from Freudian dogma, threatening Freud with heresy from his anointed heir; and this heir's wobbly support of Freud in his battle against Adler's apostasy. One can sense in Jung's convoluted attempts to explain himself to Freud the alarm he felt during this period each time he opened a letter from Vienna. Trying to soothe Freud by decrying Stekel's "utter irresponsibility" in taking Adler's side—"merely because they have the same complexes" —he hinted between the lines that he was beginning to weigh, not so unconsciously, the whole issues of alliance, loyalty, and conflict of opinion—issues that were about to come to the fore in his own relationship with Freud. Not yet ready for an open break, Jung would be provocative and appeasing in turn. Freud's more masochistic moods seemed to feed Jung's rebelliousness; when Freud stood firm or counterattacked, Jung tended to fall back into obsequiousness.

Jung's uneasiness increased when Freud intimated in August 1911 that he was about to invade Jung's preserve of the psychology of religion. Freud's letter informing him of this new venture was so Jungian in its obfuscation that Jung was at a loss, at first, what to make of it. He had even consulted Emma, he wrote back, to "unriddle" the master's "anagrams." In the process, he had reached surmises which, for the time being, he probably ought to keep to himself. The last remark echoed a hint in Freud's letter that in his new pursuits he had unearthed most uncanny things which he would "almost feel obliged *not* to discuss" with Jung.

When Freud confirmed that he was indeed investigating the psychological roots of religion, Jung dejectedly concluded that in this field too Freud would outdistance him, but his gloom was replaced by rage when Freud, misreading some of his remarks, congratulated him for coming to adopt notions about the origin of religious feelings that were completely at odds with the views Jung actually held. Feeling misunderstood, and perhaps even mocked, Jung informed Freud that he was intensifying his offensive against Freud's libido theory, a most vulnerable part of the Freudian system. Freud replied—how sincerely?—that he was pleased about Jung's attack on this thorny question and expected "much light" from it. But he also cautioned Jung not to let misunderstandings, theoretical or other, drive a wedge between them. The tone of Freud's letters during this period (late 1911) is that of a man fighting desperately against his own and Jung's rage. Wishfully misjudging the true state of affairs, Freud noted: ". . . opposition is strengthening the ties between us. . . ."

Under the pressure of the gathering storm, Jung's letters became even more convoluted. He would apologize ceaselessly for being remiss and empty-handed in his letters. He went so far as to denounce himself as an "irresponsible" correspondent. Freud, stung by Jung's neglect, was not mollified by such self-accusations. Stating that "irresponsible" was a vague moralistic label which psychoanalysts ought to dispense with, he insisted that Jung's silences must have deeper causes. He, Freud, in any case, had taken the precaution of turning off his "excess libido." Jung in his reply accused himself of further faults, of being "awkward" and "nasty," but then reminded Freud of his value as an apostle of psychoanalysis who would never have taken on this apostolic mission in the first place had heresy not run in his blood. Emboldened by this assertion of congenital heresy, he went on to pluck at Freud's "laurels" a bit, though he hid behind Nietzsche's *Zarathustra* in doing so: "One repays a teacher badly if one remains only a pupil."

In the process of de-Freudening himself, Jung now began to revise another of Freud's key concepts—his Oedipal derivation of the incest taboo. Jung "improved" the Freudian theories about this matter to the point where they exactly reversed Freud's statements. In Jung's new view, the incest taboo, far from originating in the need to master the fatalities of Oedipal passions (as Freud taught), was rather a symbolic ceremony of atonement, neither Oedipal nor even specifically sexual in its origins; its main function, Jung held, was to neutralize the intense but diffuse anxiety of primitive man. Jung saw the Oedipal yearnings as arising from, rather than giving rise to, the incest taboo; it was precisely the prohibition of incest which gave incestuous yearnings their peculiar virulence—the virulence of lusting after the now forbidden fruit. To "prove" his point, Jung noted that by the time the son was physically strong enough to challenge his father, the mother "with her sagging belly and varicose veins" could hardly any longer constitute a very desirable sexual prize. This argument sounds so incredibly hollow and superficial in its literal commitment to physical attributes that it points to what must have been a very sore spot in Jung's personal history.

Freud's reaction was predictable. The alleged innovations—advanced in a style whose confusion was compounded by Jung's fear of offending—struck Freud as "regressive"; they seemed merely to regurgitate views psychoanalysis had already exploded. In his vexation, Freud pointed to "fatal" similarities between Jung's pseudonovelties and Adler's tenets.

Jung experienced the comparison with Adler as "a bitter pill." He had also detected other signs of Freud's growing displeasure. Yet, convinced that the reasons for his theoretical divergencies with Freud were "not frivolous," he stood fast. His Swiss obstinacy, he noted, left him no choice but to go his own way for a while.

With personal acrimony invading their theoretical arguments, the conflict might have come to a head at this point if Jung had not physically removed himself from the scene by traveling once more to the U.S. (September to November 1911). He had been invited by Fordham University to give some evening lectures on psychoanalysis. A letter to Freud stated that he had accepted the invitation "so as to gain yet more ground for psychoanalysis." Yet his Fordham lectures emphasized his differences with Freud. In particular, he soft-pedaled and disavowed the Freudian theory of infantile sexuality. After his return, he wrote Freud that his shrewd playing-down of the sexual factor had converted many Americans, who would otherwise have been put off, to psychoanalysis. Freud's frosty reply was that Jung could have gained additional converts by retreating even further from psychoanalysis.

Earlier, Jung might have reacted to such a rebuke with

expiatory breast-beating. Yet with the applause of his American audiences still ringing in his ears, he struck a bolder note. He was tired, he wrote Freud, of bearing the brunt of Freud's resentment, tired of seeing his theoretical misgivings reduced to neurotic quirks, tired of being treated like "a fool riddled with complexes." Mentioning for the first time a possible break with Freud, he averred such a rupture *not* necessary provided Freud was ready to be more "objective."

As their friendship disintegrated, the two men kept protesting to each other—and to third parties—that it was not endangered. In the fall of 1912, shortly before the final break, Freud wrote Ernest Jones that a rupture between him and Jung was unlikely. In November of that year, the two men met for the last time. The meeting took place in Munich where a few leading psychoanalysts had gathered to discuss business matters. Freud and Jung had a long private talk during which harmony was apparently restored. Once more, Jung did most of the yielding, admitting to various faux pas and being suitably contrite. Freud was triumphant but suffered a sudden fainting fit during the ensuing luncheon.

In a subsequent letter to Jung, Freud attributed the fainting spell to physical causes—a migraine headache—but conceded that "a bit of neurosis" might also have played a part. In the same letter, Freud announced a forthcoming review of Jung's libido paper by another psychoanalyst and then proceeded to congratulate Jung for a "great," if unintended, "revelation" contained in this paper. According to Freud, Jung had unwittingly shown that mysticism was a byproduct of decaying neurotic complexes.

Jung, who did not think he had shown anything of the kind, saw red. In his rage, he now attacked Freud personally and accused him of being too neurotic to do justice to the work of others. Caustically, he apologized for being at times afflicted with the "purely human" wish to be understood intellectually rather than relentlessly psychoanalyzed. Freud's caustic science, he noted, was used by his supine followers to dismiss and devalue opponents. Jung himself had been victimized by such evil simplemindedness; "someone" (did he suspect Freud?) had cooked up the theory that Jung's libido concept was a symptom of anal eroticism. This sort of wretched "theorizing," the reduction of every criticism to neurotic complexes, made Jung fear for the future of psychoanalysis. Freud's own authoritarianism, Jung now reminded his mentor, had been blatantly revealed during their trip to America; at the time, Freud had broken off their mutual analysis through fear of losing his authority. Lest his Helvetic bluntness be misunderstood, Jung hastened to add, he was writing to Freud as a *friend* (underlined by Jung): "This is *our* style." (In contrast to the "depreciatory," "devaluing" style of the Viennese, which, during the Nazi period, will be called "Jewish-corrosive.")

Freud's reply was rather restrained. Yet a couple of letters later, he could not resist a taunt about a slip of the pen Jung had made regarding cronyism, Adler, and Freud. Whereupon Jung, in a paroxysm of rage, escalated his unsolicited psychoanalysis of Sigmund Freud. Prefacing his remarks with, "If you doubt my words, so much the worse for you," Jung now accused Freud of misusing analysis to transform his pupils into "slavish sons or insolent puppies." By reducing everyone around him to the level of sons and daughters who blushingly confess their mistakes, Freud was maintaining his position on top as the almighty father. But Jung was no longer taken in by

Freud's "little tricks." His own symptomatic slips, he wrote, were nothing compared to the formidable beam (of neurosis) in his brother Freud's eye. In fact, he himself, Jung sang out, was "not in the least neurotic—touch wood!" For he had been through analysis, to which Freud had refused to submit—with predictable results. Coarsely telling Freud that one does not get very far with mere self-analysis, Jung asked him to descend from his lofty perch and really come to grips with his own weak spots for a change. If Freud was willing to do so, Jung would root out his ambivalence toward him. In the meantime, he would continue telling Freud, in private, what he really thought of him (thus admitting, indirectly, to years of hypocrisy). Once more Jung insisted that his bluntness was a token of his friendship.

Freud was unsure about how to deal with this peculiar token. He at first drafted a rather meek reply, defending himself against Jung's reproach that he was exploiting psychoanalysis to keep his followers in a state of dependency. Freud did not mail this apologetic note; instead he forwarded a stiff-necked reply, rejecting Jung's accusations as "demonstrably untrue." With pained dignity, he reminded Jung of the convention among analysts "that none of us need feel ashamed of his own bit of neurosis." By claiming to be in perfect health, while behaving oddly, Jung was giving grounds to the suspicion that he lacked insight into his own illness. His last letter had created an impossible situation; hence it seemed best to "abandon our personal relations entirely."

Freud's letter of rupture crossed with a letter from Jung extending New Year's wishes for 1913. In a conciliatory gesture, he offered to discontinue his "secret" letters if Freud found them too vexing. But he insisted on his right to reciprocity, his right to treat Freud with the same "analytical considera-tion" Freud was bestowing periodically upon him. Reiterating that Freud's neurosis was to blame for his failure to grasp Jung's ideas, and protesting once more his "honorable" intentions, he left "the rest" to Freud.

Freud's letter proposing a complete break drew from Jung an oddly anemic reply. He declared himself ready to accede to Freud's wish "that we abandon our personal relations." A stilted phrase or two ("I do not thrust my friendship on any-one"), a shopworn quote from Hamlet of dubious relevance ("The rest is silence"), and an overdone display of gratitude[2] for a minor courtesy on the part of Freud completed Jung's awkward farewell.

And yet, Jung's invocation of the Danish prince's dying gasp was more than a literary flourish. The break with Freud, dreaded and wished for, was indeed a soul-shattering trauma that marked him for life. It threw him into a state of psychic desolation reminiscent of the sad years of his childhood. It shook the foundations of his being and hurtled him into a crazed agony of self-loss. It made him toil for a decade devising a typology that would transform his struggle with Freud into a matter of destiny, rooted in the fatalities of inborn character. The lacerating break with Freud, preceded by his falling-out with Bleuler and Honegger, foreboded what in old age he formulated as a law of his life: his impatience with the human frailties of others, his "fateful compulsion" to transform the arena of personal relations (especially with men) into a bat-tlefield where each of his comrades in turn had to fall and be abandoned. His heart "shamefully wrested away" by a higher

[2]Not recognizable as such in the published English translation of the letter.

power, Jung would hasten on, victim as much as sacrificer, in the grip of his imperious demon. This demon was, as demons are wont to be, two-faced. While propelling Carl Jung toward his unique visionary reality, it exacted from him a heartrending tribute of loneliness. Never was Carl Jung more wretched, never more endangered by the incubus of madness, than after his break with Sigmund Freud.

8

JOURNEY TO THE
UNDERWORLD

The break with Freud plunged Jung into an abyss. It launched him upon his "infernal journey" of self-discovery, his confrontation with the unconscious. Since Jung's ego was more brittle than Freud's, he was pulled, in exploring his psychic underworld, into chasms that Freud had managed to avoid during his self-analysis. Jung's descent into the deep brought him face to face with shapes and misshapes beyond the ken of psychoanalysis. We have already seen that Freudian dream analysis was at a loss before Jung's dreams with their rampant primitive imagery. Now, in his extremity, at the edge of madness, preyed upon by the mythological denizens of the deep, Jung had to forge singlehandedly the tools to fend off the soul-devouring demons.

In order to fight this life-and-death battle, Jung had to jettison much ballast. He withdrew from his teaching and his position at the Burghölzli asylum. He gave up reading professional journals and publishing scientific papers. He largely retreated from his few remaining friends and became even more remote than before from his family. But he never, during this lengthy crisis, relinquished his analytic work. This work, though burdensome, was vitally important to him, a lifeline anchoring him to the everyday world. His patients' struggles paralleled his own; by furthering the quest for their buried reality, he was also promoting his own self-realization.

With the ballast of external obligations, Jung also shed the conceptual baggage stifling him. He was now ready to settle his accounts—ideological and personal—with Freud. With a savagery fed by long-smoldering resentment, he now indicted psychoanalysis as a "satanic" doctrine guilty of "murdering souls." He denounced its "mania for understanding"—a mania he had shared for so long—and its "corrosive" effects on the human psyche. "The core of man," he wrote, "is a living mystery. . . ." He added that to drag this mystery into the glaring light of analysis is to sterilize it. Hence the task of the therapist is to *respect*, rather than "explain," the irrational symbols "within which the germ of life is sheltered like the seed in its hard shell." Otherwise, he becomes a purveyor of psychic violence, wrenching his charges out of their own orbits and "forcing them into foreign ones where they perish."

Whether or not he realized it, Jung was speaking here in his own behalf. He was simply reverting to the type of religiously tinged mystery that had been the focus of his experience from childhood. Looking back, he now viewed his conversion to psychoanalysis as tantamount to mental rape, the more shameful for his collusion. Jung was certain—with a certainty born of despair—that he must backtrack to restore the continuity of his life. He was too near the abyss of madness to be overly fastidious about his means of escape.

After the failure of many attempts to conjure up his purloined past through free association, an "impulse from the unconscious" prompted Jung to venture upon a new track. He suddenly remembered how, when he was ten or eleven, he would become totally absorbed, for days and weeks on end, in building castles, towers, and gates with wooden blocks. This memory stirred up strong emotion. Here, perhaps, was a point of contact with his half-dead past. Perhaps to resurrect it he had to return to the young boy engrossed in his games. That boy, he sensed, was still alive, but to reach him, through the interposed layers of time, the middle-aged Jung would have to shed his adult pride and revert to the level of the playful child. If the past would not yield to an effort of memory, Jung would literally have to reenact it.

Today, we no longer see anything unusual in this sort of active play therapy. But in Jung's era of starched collars, of solemn masculine dignity (especially among professional men), a deliberate surrender to childish things was a bizarre, almost desperate step. In fact, the thirty-eight-year-old Jung felt deeply humiliated by this abdication. Yet he was quickly rewarded. The frozen stream of his imagination thawed. His unconscious, prodded into action, spewed forth a profusion of dreams and waking visions which shed a flickering light upon the darkness of his confusion.

During the early stage of the crisis—fall and winter 1913—most of Jung's visions were of a terrifying nature. He was haunted by the recurrent specter of enormous yellow waves drowning countless thousands and turning into a crimson sea of blood. At other times, he saw thick, seemingly inexhaustible founts of blood gushing from the earth. After these visions of blood subsided, he had repeated nightmares in which intense cold invaded the earth from outer space and froze all life. Such apocalyptic visions often herald the outbreak of virulent psychosis; Jung chose to see them, in retrospect, as harbingers of World War I, then about to erupt.

Did Jung realize, then or later, how close he came to the catastrophe of complete self-loss? We do not know for sure. His later comments about this period are contradictory, though tending to play down the degree of his pathology. His repeated references to the daily routine of his analytic work as his savior during those dark years indicate some awareness of the danger he was running. (He also mentioned his family life as a redeeming factor, but this was mostly window-dressing.) During the supreme crisis of his self-confrontation, Jung, the wounded healer, did benefit from his psychiatric experience. His long intimacy with schizophrenia may have "immunized" him, to a degree, against its more extreme ravages. Also Jung's boldness in dealing with his volcanic unconscious was tempered with a goodly dose of caution: if his plunge into the inferno was less under his control than he imagined, he was circumspect enough to maintain a lifeline to the world above. Tethered thus, he could endure the surrealness of his visions without losing his grip on everyday reality.

When, toward the close of 1913, Jung finally yielded to the explosive forces within and leaped into the inner abyss, he recognized that the jump—which was more of a fall—was risky, but he was unclear as to the exact nature of this risk. The bloody visions clouding his waking hours were obviously meant as warnings from his unconscious. What was amiss? What was expected from him? He felt at a loss, not knowing in which direction to turn. Once again, his dreams came to the rescue.

A "great dream" obligingly presented itself at the eve of Christmas 1913. In this dream, Jung joined a swarthy hunting companion, who had something savage about him, in murdering Siegfried, hero of the Nibelung legend. The setting: the high mountain ranges; the time: the hour of sunrise. When the two companions spotted Siegfried on a ridge—a horn proclaiming his approach—both shot off their guns at the same time. The Germanic hero collapsed, mortally wounded, and the dark-skinned savage delivered the coup de grace. Jung could not bear to watch. Horrified, driven by disgust and fear of discovery, he ran off in search of a place to hide. He had to choose between two paths of flight, one descending to the valley below, the other climbing higher into the mountains. As he labored upward, a heavy rain began that would erase all traces of the murder. But as Jung's fear of being found out subsided, his feelings of guilt became unbearable.

At first, Jung could make little of this dream. Yet he felt that his sanity, perhaps his survival, hinged on his success in decoding it. After racking his brain to no purpose, he finally hit upon the idea that Siegfried, the murdered hero, must embody Jung's own "heroism," his brittle self-assertion. The starched willfulness that had ruled his life for so long was obsolete and had to die. The swarthy savage who had finished off Siegfried was, in turn, seen to represent a potential in Jung's unconscious, about to burst into actuality. The whole dream mirrored a violent inner upheaval, the revolt of the enslaved self against the dominion of the will.

By reading the dream in this way, Jung managed to calm his

anguish. But he failed to see how solipsistic and "Jungian" his interpretation actually was. He had fallen into the trap that invariably dooms attempts at self-analysis, seeing in the dream only what he wanted to see. Oblivious to his blind spot, caught in a narrow world of shadows, viewing each dream image as merely another facet of himself, he was able to mitigate the terrible impact of outer reality—at the price of reducing his contact with it.

Turning inward, Jung tried to disarm the external world. In the process he created a vacuum which was soon filled by spirits. These spirit figures, endowed with a reality of their own, had individualized personalities; they spoke to Jung and answered his questions; in short, they were quite as vivid to him as the ghost was to Hamlet. Was Jung, then, "hallucinating"? Yes, he was, if we want to describe his experience in clinical jargon. But this jargon is loaded and implies that these experiences are pathological. That hallucinations are, in fact, symptoms of mental illness was, a generation ago, nearly an axiomatic truth. If this truth of yesterday has become at best a half-truth today, we owe this change in no small way to Carl Jung.

The figure of Carl Jung is living proof that even in the twentieth century a person can be a visionary, "hallucinating" ghosts and demons, without being manifestly mad. Therein lies part of his importance for us now. Too productive and articulate to be dismissed as a mere lunatic, Jung had the good fortune to discover ways to reconcile his visionary experiences with the demands of external reality. True, his (or his wife's) wealth eased these demands. It nevertheless required courage to see creative potential in what others shrank from as "madness"—the courage to do without the restrictive (and protective) blinders of common sense.

The tools with which Jung mastered the visions welling up from his unconscious were deceptively simple. Besides using his "play therapy," he made certain to record his dreams and fantasies in minute detail, drawing or painting them whenever possible. He also endeavored to "amplify" the tissue of his visions by drawing upon the rich storehouses of mythology and folktales. His main goal was to objectify, and then confront, the products of his unconscious.

These visions and dreams were recorded in the so-called "Red Book," a thick folio bound in red leather. They were set down in a solemn, antiquarian style in fancy calligraphy, and adorned with equally solemn, self-conscious illustrations. In later years, Jung was quite critical of the precious style of this journal. And indeed, looking at the stiff, mannered drawings, we realize that he did well not to take his artistic ambitions too seriously.

At the beginning of the Red Book, Jung noted that having achieved, by his late thirties, the fame, wealth, knowledge, and power he had yearned for in his youth, he must now turn inward, to serve the "spirit of the depths." Only thus would he be able to repossess his soul, which he had forfeited by making it the object of rational-scientific inquiry. "I failed to consider that the soul cannot be the object of my judgment and knowledge; rather, my judgment and knowledge are the objects of my soul." The soul is primary—an independent, living entity—the antecedent, and foundation, of all our psychology.

One of the first figures Jung encountered during his descent to the underworld was "Philemon," an old man with bull's horns and the wings of a kingfisher. He was a kind of Gnostic, a teacher of spiritual enlightenment, who appeared to Jung in many waking visions and dreams. In long talks, Philemon instructed Jung about the dark realms beyond the ken of the conscious ego. He seemed to Jung almost "physically real," even walking with him in the garden. Jung later described this peripatetic spirit as an embodiment of the "wise old man"—an archetype that Jung himself, with advancing age, strove to approximate.

Philemon—winged, but lame in one foot—represented what Jung had looked for, apparently found, and then tragically lost in Freud: paternal wisdom and guidance, readiness to minister to his spiritual needs. Jung's flesh-and-blood father had failed him in this respect; so had Bleuler, Janet, and Flournoy. Now the role of spiritual father had fallen to a figure from the spirit world, imperishable but essentially impalpable, and with this ersatz, Jung had to be content. In later years, when he felt downcast, Jung sometimes lamented that he had not been permitted to find the living, breathing guru for whom every fiber of his being had yearned.

Philemon was also closely linked with Jung's pervasive sense of guilt. The tragic fate of Philemon and Baucis, as depicted in Goethe's *Faust*, was a lifelong preoccupation of Jung's. In this drama, Faust in his arrogance has the innocent old couple, who are in the way of his grandiose schemes, killed. The immense burden of guilt Faust incurs as a result of this murder was paralleled in Jung's feelings toward his parents. Over the years, he tried to atone for this guilt by becoming the advocate and avenger of Philemon and Baucis. Having initially identified with the Faustian superman, he later rallied to the cause of the victims of that overweening pride. In his forties, Jung chiseled into the stone wall of his tower retreat in Bollingen: *"Philemon sacrum—Fausti poenitentia"* (Philemon's shrine—Faust's penitence). Some twenty-five years later, Jung said in a letter that his role as avenger of Philemon had become, as it were, a "personal matter" between himself and the "proavus Goethe." This unusual written reference to the legend of his descent from Goethe, with its self-conscious use of the Latin term for ancestor, reveals how emotionally charged Jung's Philemon complex actually was. Two years after this letter, when a serious illness left him a semi-invalid, Jung began to refer to himself, with a note of bitterness, as "the limping messenger from the lake." Like Philemon he was now physically lame, dependent on the wings of the spirit.

During the crisis years, along with the wise and benevolent Philemon, another spirit voice gained great importance. This was a female voice with a ring of dazzling ambiguity, seductive and fateful. Jung easily recognized it as that of a patient then under his care. He described this woman as a "talented psychopath" who was smitten with him. There is little doubt, however, that Jung himself at times succumbed to a fascination for this female figure who—boldly and without warning—had made herself heard within him. In typical fashion, Jung tried to distance her by divesting her of her individuality. He resolved that this patient as such was fortuitous, a poor accidental creature whose function was merely to serve as a vehicle of symbolic content. She had provided Jung with a blank screen on which to project a female aspect of himself: the "anima," as he came to call it. This radical sort of depletion, which reduces individuals to amorphous, vapid "functionaries" while parading as enrichment, henceforth becomes characteristic of Jungian psychology. We can clearly see here how Jung's own pathology—his phobia of being "invaded" and his distrust of women—determined the form of his psychological doctrine.

The message this "anima" wanted to get across was that Jung's psychology of the unconscious belonged much more to art than science. This message hit a raw nerve. Jung had grown used to being denounced as a "mystic" by Freudians and others, but now his own anima wanted to exile him to the domain of the esthetic, calling into question the objective validity of his painstakingly amassed findings. This was the more intolerable as Jung was actually attracted to the realm of the arts while acutely aware of his own lack of artistry. The belief in the "scientific" validity of his work was vital to him. Hence the crafty insinuations of the anima struck at the very roots of his being.

With a stubbornness clearly tied to deep doubts about the validity of his own person, Jung insisted, again and again, that he was a "scientist." He fought tooth and nail against the anima's attempts to enlist him in the ranks of artistry. Ever suspicious of the female and of her demonic powers, Jung saw the anima as rising out of the primal ooze, infested with "all the slimy and monstrous appurtenances of the deep." In order to limit her fatal power, Jung proceeded to shift the value emphasis of his doctrine. By reinstating consciousness, at the expense of the unconscious, as the psyche's ultimate authority, he strove to reduce the dominion of the demonic female.

The danger in yielding to the siren songs of the femme fatale was demonstrated to Jung by the example of his cousin and colleague Franz Riklin. The latter had been persuaded by the same woman patient that he was a misunderstood artist, with the result that he neglected his family and his psychiatric work, started drinking heavily, and gradually went to seed. Jung saw him as a victim of the "abysmal cunning" of the anima, who could "totally destroy" a vulnerable man.

His cousin's plight fortified Jung's resolve not to give in to the anima. He told her outright that she had missed the mark in regarding the forms rising from his unconscious as creations of art, that, on the contrary, they were spontaneous products of nature, autonomous, beyond the control of his will. What followed was an endlessly repetitive argument of the sort often staged by children, with both parties stubbornly clinging to their own viewpoints. At length, however, the dispute became a dialogue and Jung began to discover positive aspects of the anima he had previously overlooked.

Jung's dealings with this intangible presence soon grew so intense that he felt as if he were in analysis with a female spirit. Compared to a human therapist, the anima had the advantage of not charging a fee. But as she was out to spin intrigues, Jung thought it prudent to communicate with her in writing. In this way, she would find it more difficult to distort his messages to her. (Even as a schoolboy, Jung had written advance alibis to be used later in countering accusations made by teachers or peers.) Unfortunately, Jung did not reveal how the anima reacted to his vote of no confidence.

Jung did manage to escape the fate of his cousin Riklin, perhaps because of his cautiousness. During the crisis years still to come, however, it was the fate of another man—whom he also saw as a victim of the unconscious, and with whom he had identified since adolescence—that Jung was terrified of recapitulating. This man was Friedrich Nietzsche. Even in his student days, Jung had not been able to read *Zarathustra* without experiencing shivers of fright. And even then he was tormented by a secret fear that he might grow to resemble the deranged philosopher. (Nietzsche—like Carl Jung a minister's son—had taught at the University of Basel when Carl was a child.) The student Carl Jung had compared *Zarathustra*, exploding from the volcano of Nietzsche's unconscious, to the discovery of his own self Number Two. Afraid that he might share the philosopher's pathology, he brooded on whether it was possible to confront the inner demons without being sucked into the maelstrom of insanity. The conclusion he reached was that Nietzsche had been guilty of a monumental folly by offering his profound intimations of the ineffable to an "obtuse, God-forsaken crowd" of Philistines. Nietzsche's fatal flaw, in the eyes of the medical student Carl Jung, was his lack of secretiveness.

In the fateful years after 1913, Jung himself experienced the onslaught of the unconscious. Barely escaping psychic destruction, he realized that the fury of the unchained demons could not be appeased by mere secretiveness, that much more potent countermeasures were needed. Jung felt at a distinct advantage vis-à-vis the restless, wind-blown Nietzsche, in that he had firm social roots. Was Toni Wolff—the ex-patient who became his lover and "femme inspiratrice"—by then an important link to social reality? Did she, Ariadne-like, help him to thread his way out of the labyrinth of psychic aberration? We do not know. Jung was rather secretive on this point, preferring to credit his methods of exorcism through art for his salvation. Be that as it may, a sort of integration took place when split facets of his personality began to coalesce into coherent figures like "Philemon" and "Anima." From a clinical perspective, such a consolidation has distinct pathognomic features. They were outweighed, however, in Jung's case, by the positive aspect: the surmounting of a dangerously unstable, amorphous phase of personality development. After his protracted skirmishes with the anima, in any event, Jung's inner state gradually stabilized. Though he continued to feel the tug of the spirit world, he was now safe from being swallowed by it. The process of personification proved to be a magical act; calling the spirits by name, Jung could hold them in check.

By 1918, the crisis that had lasted nearly six years and culminated at the brink of insanity had abated. Around this time, Jung began to discover a mysteriously veiled, yet unmistakable trend within the apparent chaos of his inner images. His dreams became more concise and defined, as did the paintings he produced at the behest of his unconscious. Increasingly, his pictures assumed circular or quadratic forms, highly geometrical. Basing himself on Indian models, Jung called them mandalas. In his view, the mandalas were cryptograms of an inner centering process, reflecting a scheme of order inherent in the psyche. The mandala's magic circle or square, symbolic of harmony and balanced completion, was a paradigm of the goal of psychic development: bringing buried material to consciousness until consciousness and the unconscious are in balance. Jung viewed the self as the psychic equivalent of the mandala. The devious and meandering path to self-discovery he called individuation. Individuation, based on a delicate, dynamic synthesis of conscious and unconscious, designated henceforth both the goal of Jungian therapy and the method for its attainment. The mandala-number "four" became Jung's sacred number, the quaternity, his ordering principle. It encompassed all psychology and all of reality. (Inevitably, this cosmic scheme had something Procrustean about it.)

With the personification and naming of the anima, forerunner of Jung's mythology of the archetypes; with the technique of "active imagination," evoking and solidifying the dark emanations of the unconscious; with the symbol of the mandala and the concept of individuation, Jung had found not only the rudiments of a solution to his personal crisis, but also the lineaments of a far-reaching doctrine, a doctrine perhaps not as original as it claims to be, but speaking with a voice decidedly its own.

Thus Jung's infernal journey proved fruitful in the end. The man who had endured its perils emerged stronger and more autonomous than before. No longer suited to be the disciple and understudy of another, he was now ready to step forth as the herald of his own doctrine, shaped by the quasi-psychotic experience of his years in the wilderness.

It was not frivolous opportunism, as his detractors suspected, that moved Jung to cast himself as spokesman for spirituality and for the "reality of the soul." If his occasional cynicism encouraged such suspicions, the deadly earnest with which he threw himself into this cause, as if singled out by fate, is unmistakable. He remained loyal to this fateful mission all of his life; and though he strenuously denied any ambition to be a prophet or the evangelist of a new religion, Jung did perceive his message of the soul's reality as a *religious* matter. In his relentless service to the soul, Carl Jung was taking up, once again, the task left unfinished by his father, a task which he himself apparently abandoned when he turned to the study of medicine. Also, he was reestablishing continuity with his own childhood history and his maternal line of descent.

9

TONI WOLFF—
EROS-WINGED MUSE

The middle-aged Jung had a rugged, powerful physique. His squat body, hardly marked by the passing years, could have been that of a farmer or forester, perhaps also of a miner who drills underground shafts and dynamites rock quarries. There was something rough-hewn and coarse about him, about his brisk but graceless movements, his pseudojovial bearing. The head atop this bearlike figure was massive, high-domed, with sharp cunning eyes in a face whose firm, almost obstinate set seemed to reflect an undercurrent of rage. As a whole, Jung's physical appearance in those years was oddly inconsistent; it lacked balance—as did his work.

This dissonance was reflected in Jung's social awkwardness, in the frequent coarseness of his table talk, and the pedantry of much of his writing for public consumption. (His letters, though, when he dropped his posturing, could be engagingly direct.) He attempted to hide his social clumsiness behind a pose of nonchalance that reeked of affectation. The booming guffaws that became his trademark were part of this act; so was the sarcasm he poured upon the just and unjust alike. His suppressed rage was vented, deviously, in the underhandedness of the practical joker.

Jung's massive figure required constant motion. The long hours of sitting still imposed by his analytical work were physical torture for him. When the weather was fine, he liked to receive his patients in the garden behind his house, where he could stroll about with them. The idea of a peripatetic therapy, of an analyst who thought with his body as well as his head, appealed to him. In his restlessness, he fiddled constantly with his pipe. (Long after his health had forced him to give up smoking, he would, with a sad mien, turn and twist an empty pipe in his hands.)

His strong hands delighted in all manner of art work. Jung loved to draw and paint, to sculpt and chisel stone, to do masonry work. Sturdy as an ox, he could carry heavy bags of cement and chop wood for hours at a time. Yet despite this physical ruggedness, there was something fragile about him, as if the frail figure of old age were already shadowing the massive man of forty-five. His emotional frailty was painfully evident, though he tried to mask it with a tough arrogance.

This toughness veered at times toward brutality and could assume peculiar forms. When a woman tormented by a syphilis phobia consulted Jung, he reviled her as a "filthy swine" who sullied him with her presence and ordered her from his house. The Jungian recounting the anecdote applauded this "master-

ful cruelty" which "by playing along with the patient's masochism, jolts her out of it." Another devout Jungian reported
that the master's "apparent cruelties" toward her invariably
promoted her inner growth. Shortly before the death of Richard Wilhelm, whose fatal illness touched Jung deeply, he remarked that Wilhelm might just as well die; after all, he had
completed the "Secret of the Golden Flower" and had nothing
more to give.

This callousness was bound to injure vulnerable natures. To
what extent it contributed to the suicides of Honegger and
others of Jung's circle is an open question. Some of this manner
rubbed off on Jung's disciples. Frances Wickes, an early American follower of his, once remarked that for a while she had been
troubled by the number of suicides and premature deaths
among people analyzed by Jungians. Later, however, she had
come to realize that "integration alone matters, even if it does
not come about in this life. . . ."

Despite his protracted self-analysis Jung had not come to
terms with his deeper emotions, and the feeling side of his
personality remained undeveloped. This emotional stiffness
was felt keenly by his family, and by friends and colleagues. Yet
admiring patients and disciples (the two categories overlap, his
early followers being mostly former patients) experienced a
different Jung—warm, paternal, caring. Apparently Jung could
radiate sympathy when its display did not obligate him much.
But his emotional constriction was his weak spot. One is
tempted to apply the psychosomatic notions which Jung applied so freely to others (but seldom to himself): perhaps his
emotional tightness was closely linked to the cardiac illness
which would first "bust" (Jung's term) and then kill him.

This atrophy of feeling was oppressive for those who did not unreservedly admire him. It also stifled criticism and free debate. Although he asked for the unvarnished opinions of others, they sensed he did not really mean it and held back. Jung deplored this lack of trust, not realizing that he created it. If a confrontation did arise, or threatened to, he either walked off or became overbearing. To a student at the University of Zurich who had dared to criticize him in print, Jung wrote with mock humility that he must be stupid indeed since he held only seven honorary degrees from universities such as Harvard, Yale, etc. He apparently wanted to crush this wretched midget of an opponent with the authority of his fame. Similarly, on the title page of an early work he made sure that not only M.D. but also LL.D. was included after his name. (This title was his by dint of an honorary degree.) Vanity and a yen for power were not as alien to him as he professed.

His spreading fame attracted rich Americans and Britons repelled by the crudities of Freudian analysis. The lofty spirituality of the Jungian school was "just the thing" for them. Used to buying the best, they settled for nothing less than the renowned head of this school. Since they disdained to learn the language of the natives, or any other alien tongue, Jung was forced to perfect his English. Fortunately, he depended less on purely verbal associations, and more on concrete imagery, than Freud.

Fame and the money it brought failed to cure Jung's *Weltschmerz.* Much of the time he was disgruntled and gloomy, sullen or irritable. He felt as much the victim as the master of the adoring band of Jung-struck Amazons that began to form around him and henceforth played Praetorian Guard at every congress and public occasion. These tokens of success struck him as essentially hollow. They hardly assuaged the pain of the inner split dating back to childhood and reflected, to the end of his days, in the duality of his life-style and his morose moods.

In view of this inner schism, it is hardly surprising that Jung found it necessary to divide the weight of his love life between two partners, both essential to him. If it is true that Emma's role was, by and large, to provide Carl with the motherliness he missed in his own mother, then it is also evident that he needed to seek other, less regressive ties outside his marriage. It was only a matter of time before a woman would emerge to fill this vacuum in Jung's life. Jung's diffidence, his fear of the femme fatale, explains why this woman first entered his sphere as a patient, young enough to touch his paternal side, and vulnerable enough to promise a lasting dependency.

Once more, Jung evolved a theory to justify his slowly deepening involvement with Toni Wolff. He theorized that there are basically two types of women: the "wife and mother" who finds fulfillment in her domesticity; and the woman destined to be mistress and "femme inspiratrice" of the creative man, sustaining him in his labors, and, in this way, partaking of his creativity. (This view implies that in the spiritual realm it is the man who fulfills the more "pregnant" maternal function.) Together these two types of women, Jung claimed, constitute the providential complement of the man of genius whose double nature requires both the earth-mother-wife and the eros-winged companion. Jung expected women to revolve like planets in the orbits prescribed by "nature" and to find happiness within these boundaries. It was convenient for him that, by and large, Emma and Toni submitted without much fussing to his imperious typecasting. Their occasional rebellions, which he saw as mutinies, were put down rather easily.

C. G. Jung—The Haunted Prophet

Born in 1888, Toni Wolff was thirteen years younger than Carl Jung. Her father, a well-to-do businessman, belonged to a patrician Zurich family. After finishing his education, he had lived for twenty years in Japan. His long exposure to Japanese culture deeply affected his outlook on life and apparently even his facial features which until his dying day retained an exotic smoothness. Upon his return to Zurich, he married a much younger woman. Soon after the birth of Toni, the oldest of three daughters, the family moved into a large villa. Toni lived there for almost sixty years.

Her education was fairly typical for a girl belonging to the wealthy bourgeoisie of that era: six years in a public primary school, followed by four years in a private girls' school, capped by the obligatory year at boarding school. Toni's lack of a formal high school diploma did not keep her from auditing courses (mostly in literature and theology) at the University of Zurich.

If the outward course of her education was standard for a girl of her background, the intensity of her intellectual pursuits was not. She received religious instruction from the reverend Oskar Pfister, the combative minister who was an early champion of Freud's cause (then not very popular) among the Swiss clergy and the public at large. Toni, very spiritual-minded, had long discussions with him and other theologians. She read a great deal and wrote lyrical poems which she never attempted to publish.

Altogether, Toni Wolff was a very private person, afraid of the limelight.[1] This deerlike shyness remained with her throughout her life; it was hardly dented by her becoming

---

[1] Her sister Erna Naeff was sure she was acting according to Toni's wishes by burning, after the latter's sudden death, her extensive correspondence with Carl Jung.

president of the Psychological Club. Only in her sixties did she dare give regular public lectures. The austere reserve that made her freeze in the presence of uncongenial people was often interpreted by others as arrogance. It was, in fact, this shyness which led her to consult, at her mother's instigation, the psychiatrist Carl Jung.

Toni first saw Carl Jung around the time of the death of her father, who had been a stranger to her. That was in 1909 when Toni was twenty-one. We don't know much about her symptoms and the course of her treatment. Jung later described her to a friend as a schizophrenic he had cured. The accuracy of this diagnosis is open to question. What is certain, though, is that Toni blossomed under Jung's care.

The informality with which Jung conducted his therapy— a far cry from the stiffness of orthodox psychoanalysis—favored the growth of friendship among doctor and patient. At times, Jung seemed to invite such developments and the attendant risks to therapy. He was not averse to mingling with patients socially. He once confided to Ernest Jones that he was reluctant to probe too deeply into the seamier side of his patients' sexuality because it would be embarrassing for both parties were they later to face each other across a dinner table.

Some of the reasons for the mutual attraction between Carl Jung and Toni Wolff are obvious; others can be easily guessed at. It is not hard to intuit how Toni must have felt toward the man to whom she owed her health or, at least, a life that was bearable. Through him, she felt herself affirmed and validated. His far-ranging mind opened new intellectual horizons for her. In short, Carl Jung furthered her growth and gave her the spiritual guidance her father had failed to provide—an almost irresistible form of seduction. Besides, Jung was tangibly a man of stature, full of vitality, successful, sensitive, and animated by a creative fire which tended to fascinate intellectually starved women. Next to this Faustian figure, the reverends and university professors, who had up to then occupied Toni's fantasies, seemed rather anemic.

Also Toni must have sensed pretty soon, if Jung did not say so outright, that the life of this active, successful man, surrounded by a large family, lacked warmth. Jung felt lonely, then and later, and did not try to conceal this feeling. He felt orphaned, both emotionally and intellectually, after the tie to Freud was severed and after friends like Alphonse Maeder and Franz Riklin, with whom he had sought solace, disappointed him. As he advanced into middle age, the thought of giving intellectual knowledge for erotic warmth must have occurred to him, as it does to many middle-aged intellectuals. And here was a young, attractive, well-educated woman who seemed to absorb each of his words with fierce passion and who needed him deeply. Was not one of the first visions during his night journey through the unconscious the double image of Elias and Salome, the wizened old man and the erotic young girl? It is true that this pairing had bothered him at first, in spite of Elias' assurances that he and Salome had belonged to each other since the beginning of time. Only later, Jung wrote, had he come to understand the union of the old man and the young woman, the fusion of knowledge and eros, as perfectly natural.

We may surmise that Jung's ingrained distrust vis-à-vis the "demonic cunning" of Eros in female guise—a cunning which, in Jung's words, "can utterly ruin" a susceptible man—was not easily overcome by Toni's presence. It was probably Toni who (shyly) encouraged a deepening closeness between them, while Jung was happy to receive her attentions. (An amiable passivity in the face of adulation from female admirers was characteristic of him and became more marked with advancing age.) In Toni's case, the danger of female power was attenuated by her virginal innocence, vulnerability, and her thirst for instruction.

One has to visualize Jung's situation at the time he gradually discovered in Toni his "soror mystica"—as overly delicate Jungians called her. It was the time of deep inner disarray, of his lonely confrontation with his unconscious. It was the time when he was suffering from the aftermath of his traumatic break with Freud and when he began to perceive the "brutal reality" behind the mirages of marriage. In his case, this brutal reality resided in the inexorable fact that Emma, no matter how generous and giving, would never be able to make up for the emotional deficit of Carl's childhood. And to the extent that she became a maternal figure, she automatically disqualified herself as Salome, as erotic counterpart. This impossibility of making mother and sexual lover coincide in one woman—an attempt which dooms so many neurotic marriages—constituted the secret tragedy of Carl Jung's married life.

For a long time, Carl refused to acknowledge this painful truth. He might be bold and even reckless in the realm of ideas, but in the conduct of his daily life he was far from being an adventurer. He did not want to jeopardize his marriage and his family life. But he also knew that he was not happy, and he was not old and resigned enough to locate the roots of his unhappiness inside himself. And thus when faced by this young woman who owed her spiritual life to him, who ached to share the flights of his imagination, who looked up to him as a demigod, and who, moreover, radiated the nymphlike sensuality often found in girls living at the edge of madness—when all this beckoned, was it really surprising that Jung found it increasingly hard to resist, and that he finally recognized this touching, enticingly vulnerable figure as *his* Salome, and appropriated her?

His growing involvement with Toni Wolff precipitated a stormy marital crisis. Emma felt hurt and angry. Her territory was encroached upon, and she resented the intruder. But her situation was difficult. Toni was not an anonymous siren, an unscrupulous seductress, to whom Emma could impute the worst of motives and against whom she could freely vent her righteous indignation. Toni was a friend, almost a member of the Jung family; she accompanied the Jungs on their travels and nursed them when they were sick. Emma could not simply be oblivious to Toni's thoughtful sensitivity. Besides, Emma was not the kind of woman who would fight with any weapon at her command. In the fight against Toni, her freedom to maneuver was severely limited.

Carl Jung at first reacted to this entanglement and to the pain he was causing his wife with a penitent despondency which he tried to smother by insisting upon his right to amplify his life. But he did not allow himself in the long run to be deflected by Emma's reproaches or by his own scruples, and ultimately the lengthy, at times bitter, struggle ended with his victory: Emma accepted the triangular situation; Carl could keep both his mistress and his family.

Jung's affair with Toni might have been less troublesome if he had not insisted on drawing his mistress into his family life and on having her as a regular guest for Sunday dinner. Did he do this because he wanted to fragment his life as little as possible, because he detested the hypocrisy of a clandestine affair, or for other reasons? We do not know. Whatever his motives, his endeavors to make his family accept Toni succeeded only in part. His children, in particular, showed little sympathy for the sensitive "Aunt Toni" and often teased her unmercifully.

Despite these difficulties, Jung managed to maintain this asymmetrical triangle for several decades, drafting both women to serve his cause. Thus, Emma Jung was the first president of the Jungian "Psychological Club"; a few years after she resigned, Toni assumed the presidency. Both women published papers about Jungian psychology. Patients whom Jung wanted to refer to a female therapist were sometimes told to "see either my wife or Miss Toni Wolff." For decades Jung spent almost every Wednesday afternoon at Toni's house unless he was traveling or sick. On these Wednesdays some of Toni's relatives would often join the two for supper. The older of Toni's sisters, who was married to an architect, had undergone analysis with Jung (which, like many Jungian analyses, seems to have been rather informal and cursory) and maintained a friendship with him. Toni's younger sister was married to the psychiatrist Hans Trüb, who belonged to the inner Jung circle for years, but finally, like so many others, had a falling-out with Jung.

Jung prided himself that he managed to maintain for almost forty years the complex triangle of which he formed the apex. He considered himself a great lover, even expressed concern that this fact might escape future biographers. He relished the devotion of these two quite individualistic women, their willingness to settle for a half of Carl Jung, and their zeal to outdo each other in propagating his doctrine. And he almost managed to convince both of them that their situation was ideal. Toni even went so far as to write a treatise on female typology which was entirely based on Jungian ideas and which, like all Jungian schemas, had to be four-partite. Her four basic types were the "mother and wife," the "medial" (intermediary) woman, the "hetaera," and the "amazon." Her essay sounds as if she considered herself a mixture of the latter two.

But as subservient, and even servile, as Emma and Toni were in their endeavors to fit the roles assigned by Jung, ultimately neither of them was happy with her fate. They felt trapped in a situation which Jung declared to be "natural" but which did violence to the nature of both. They even tried to erase their rivalry by setting up regular meetings with Jung's assistant Carl A. Meier, in which they "analyzed" each other. It seems that Jung favored the formation of this curious three-some. But the conflicts between the two women were too deep-seated to be simply talked or analyzed away.

Nor could psychotherapy erase the awkwardness of Toni's social position. The role of *maîtresse attitrée* (official mistress) might have its glamorous aspects in the French or British upper classes, but in the bourgeois Zurich of the 1920s, whose moral standards were still shaped by the puritanism of Zwingli and Calvin, her social status was trying. And, as their affair went on without being legitimized, her psychological situation became trying also. Try as she might to cling to Jung's doctrine that as a "hetaera" type she was not made for marriage and child-bearing, in the end something in her rebelled. She began to demand, forcefully and gauchely, that Jung divorce Emma and marry her. Her offensive took the form of a massive direct interference in Jung's family life, which Emma could not ignore and to which Jung's children reacted by becoming even more hostile and mocking toward Aunt Toni than before.

Apparently the only one surprised by this development was Carl. He really had believed in his typology which favored his peace of mind and his digestion. Even though in his writing he had allowed for some variability of character, he had counted on his mistress remaining within the preordained category of "femme inspiratrice." Now the order of this scheme and of his personal life was unexpectedly threatened by Toni's belated marriage intentions. Luckily for Carl, however, Toni's campaign occurred at a time when his need for her had lessened and when a growing circle of younger, but no less adoring women had begun to trail after him. Also, with advancing age, Jung was less inclined than ever to give up the comfort of his home life and the still important tie to Emma for the risky move of marrying his long-time mistress. He knew of too many men who had bitterly rued such a step. A wedded muse is apt to lose her power of inspiration—particularly in the eyes of her husband. Thus, Jung found it rather easy to resist Toni's blandishments. She might still be important to him, but she was no longer indispensable.

But Carl Jung was irreplaceable for Toni. She continued to revolt intermittently against the asymmetry of their relationship, even fell in love a few times with other men, but these romances never got beyond the initial phases. Eventually, resignation made her perpetuate the role which she had seized so enthusiastically in her youth—the role of spiritual companion to Carl Jung. And even this limited role was contested by others.

Toni's last years were not serene. She smoked incessantly and drank a great deal. One of her friends said that "her heart was broken, and she did not care anymore what liquor and nicotine would do to her." Also she was plagued by a painful arthritis that she treated with very questionable methods. The pain of her barrenness would manifest itself, on occasion, in a sudden piercing coldness of her behavior. Jung detached himself gradually, seeing less and less of her. She died in the spring of 1953, at the age of sixty-four, of a heart attack. Her death seemed rather sudden, but just prior to it, she told friends that she expected her life to end soon.

Despite their estrangement, Jung was deeply affected by her death, which preceded Emma's by two years. On the day she died, and before he had been told the news, he suffered a severe heart attack. He was dismayed that her passing away found him so unprepared. A few months earlier, he had been disquieted by a number of Hades dreams but had related them to his own fate. He felt entitled to some forewarning. In a letter he noted ruefully that nobody close to Toni had had premonitory dreams, but that such dreams were reported by a number of people who had hardly known her.

10

THE PSYCHOLOGICAL CLUB

According to Jung, all his friends and colleagues left him in 1913 when he broke with Freud. (He characteristically referred to this as their "defection.") His book on the symbols of the libido pronounced hogwash and he himself decried as a "mystic," he felt as much as expelled from the scientific community. Only two friends, the psychiatrists Franz Riklin and Alphonse Maeder, stood by him.

Franz Riklin was Jung's junior by three years. He had assisted Jung with the Association Test and was connected as well by family ties, through marriage to a cousin of Jung's. Though at the time Jung generally had little use for family— *"je verwandter, je verdammter"* (the more closely related, the more intensely hated) being a pet proverb—he nonetheless patronized his cousin Riklin. When in 1910 he became president of the International Association for Psychoanalysis, Jung appointed Riklin his secretary and editor of the association's publication.

Riklin had worked in a clinic in Rheinau before he moved to Küsnacht at the urging of his wife, Jung's cousin, who was smitten with Jung and often held him up as a model to her husband. Riklin's tragedy was that he was half artist and half analyst and could not commit himself to either calling. (He was the colleague Jung mentioned who had been convinced by a woman patient—also a patient of Jung's—that he was born to be an artist, who fell for the notion and was wrecked by it.) Riklin was a friendly but rather flaccid (and henpecked) creature. For a while—around 1915—he had his own circle of pupils and ex-patients which met regularly at the café "Karl der Grosse." Toni Wolff, her sister, and her sister's husband Dr. Hans Trüb, were members. Even Jung appeared on occasion at this roundtable, where he behaved quite sarcastically and took obvious pleasure in knocking great men from their pedestals. Once, as the talk came to Abraham Lincoln, Jung informed the open-mouthed guests that Lincoln was not the great idealist he was reputed to be, that his abolitionism had been dictated by tangible political and economic interests.

Riklin, who with advancing age affected all sorts of artists' mannerisms, was a spendthrift. Deeming it narrowminded and quite beneath him to worry about money, he found himself constantly in difficult financial straits. Time and again, either directly or through his wife, he approached Jung with requests that he refer patients to him, but when the creative urge came over him his patients were compelled to sit and wait, with predictable results for his practice. With his progressive metamorphosis into a painter his financial situation deteriorated until at last it became hopeless. He had estranged himself completely from Jung in the thirties and withdrew from the Jungian Psychological Club. He died in misery a few years later.

Alphonse Maeder, the second of the two friends to stand by Jung after his break with Freud, was one of the most appealing figures in Jung's circle. He was French-Swiss, small in stature, and graceful. Charming in conversation, lucid and kind, he was modest to a fault. Jungian psychology owes him at least two of its major tenets about dreams—the interpretation on the so-called "subjective level," which relates the images of the dream directly to the dreaming subject (rather than seeking points of reference in the external world as Freud did), and the emphasis on the future-directed function of dreams. Maeder was also the source of some of the criticism leveled by Jung at psychoanalysis, but he never insisted on proprietary rights in these matters. Radiating a warmth nearly unheard of for a psychiatrist, he was revered by his patients.

Maeder's warmth thawed even Jung. He was one of a very few friends Jung made as an adult with whom he used the trusting, familiar *du* form of address. (Neither with Freud nor with his long-time assistant and coworker C. A. Meier did Jung ever use this form.) To Maeder, Jung opened his heart about his desperate struggle with the inner demons that followed his break with Freud. In gratitude for his faithful, compassionate friendship, Jung presented him in 1917 with a copy of his booklet, *Septem sermones ad mortuos*, which he had privately published under the pseudonym "Basilides." This essay he had thrown together in three evenings in a Nietzsche-esque blaze of intuition. In a covering letter to Maeder Jung described this work, which had been dictated to him as though by a host of spirits and whose setting was the "land of the dead," as a "fragment of wide-ranging connections." Since this fragment had been inspired by impersonal forces, he could not presume to sign it with his own name. In closing the letter Jung asked that Maeder guarantee the pamphlet "a discreet resting place" in his desk, where it would be safe from profane eyes.

For years, Jung was almost effusive about Maeder's virtues, but when the two became estranged during the twenties, his view of Maeder changed. From then on he was banished to the circle of those persons Jung ridiculed at the dinner table. Maeder had now become "such a dear and pious one," who did not shrink from expressing his simpleminded religious faith directly in therapy, by praying with his patients, or teaching them to pray.

In 1933, after Hitler seized power in Germany, Jung became president of the Nazified "General Medical Society for Psychotherapy"—a move which brought him much censure, as we shall see. Half a year later he invited Maeder to head a Swiss national subgroup of this society, yet to be founded. Maeder politely but firmly declined; he was too absorbed with his missionary work for the "Oxford" group for "Moral Rearmament," which he had joined of late. This refusal sat poorly with Jung, and he was soon relating an anecdote of how Maeder, during compulsory public confession in the Oxford group, confessed to the horrible sin of having worn, out of vanity, a stand-up collar so high it had chafed his neck red and bloody. Jung considered it representative of Maeder's spiritual dilletantism that he had no more interesting trespass to confess.

The year 1916, a climactic stretch in Jung's civil war with

his unconscious, was also the year in which the Jungian Psychological Club was founded. Here again one is struck by the two or even several channels of the course of Jung's life. In reading his autobiography one gets the impression that his life at the time was a social desert, consisting mainly of his solitary, wearying struggles with his demons, set alongside his work and his family duties. But his "Memories" fail to mention that he also found time, during this trying period, to help launch the first center for Jungian psychology—no small venture. It was, in fact, a rather ambitious undertaking.

True, Jung was not the moving force in this initial step of making his psychology into an institution. He simply played along with a process set in motion by others, a precedent that was repeated thirty-two years later in the founding of the C. G. Jung Institute.

In both instances it was a woman who provided the decisive impetus. The Psychological Club was the brainchild of an American, Edith Rockefeller McCormick, daughter of the founder of the Rockefeller dynasty. She was married to Harold Fowler McCormick, another member of the U. S. oligarchy, whose father had invented the reaper. Harold McCormick, who suffered manic-depressive moods, had consulted Jung in Zurich in 1908 and 1909. In 1909, when he happened to be in Vienna, he wanted to consult Freud as well but was persuaded otherwise by his wife. In a letter to Freud shortly before their joint trip to the United States in 1909, Jung expressed vexation that his "former patient McCormick" and his wife were going to cross the Atlantic aboard the same ship as he and Freud. Freud wrote back that he would protect Jung from McCormick, assuring Jung that he could be most nasty when he had to.

C. G. Jung—The Haunted Prophet

It soon became clear that McCormick was more than just a "former patient." Early in 1910 he called Jung to Chicago for further consultation because of a relapse. Jung made the long journey in a mere three weeks, two of which were consumed in traveling there and back. If one applies to Jung the standard of skepticism by which he judged the motives of others, one may assume that it was not simply humanitarian motives that made him comply with the desire of a Chicago multimillionaire for what was, in the perspective of the times, a lightning visit to the United States.

In 1915 the McCormick couple again appeared in Zurich. This time Edith McCormick also resolved to undergo analysis with Jung. That venture, an unusual one in those days for a woman of her position, apparently pleased her, for afterwards she became one of the foremost evangelists of Jungian psychology. She sought to convert a number of Freudians, skeptical artists, and other heathens, at times with a more or less gentle nudge from the dollar.

Edith McCormick's story was the typical story of the poor little rich girl. In her parents' estate she was immersed in such a welter of sharp, driving people that she had barely a minute to herself. With part of her enormous fortune, valued at one time at one hundred million dollars, she subsidized a large number of artists, often in an overbearing and capricious manner. When she disapproved of the life-style or work of one of her charges she could quite ruthlessly cut off her support, with no concern for the distress this caused the fallen favorite.

Perhaps in her Zurich exile Edith McCormick missed the "Saddle and Cycle," "Shore Acres," "Fortnightly," "Penman's," "Colony," and the numerous other clubs to which she belonged at home. In any case she came up with the notion that a club should be established for Jungian analysts, their patients, and ex-patients. Jung, who was then working on his typology, and who feared that people undergoing his brand of analysis would be too much turned inward, was attracted to the idea of a Jungian community. And it may have furthered his interest that Edith Rockefeller, as one source put it, had "sufficient means."

She did in fact make available at very short notice 360,000 Swiss francs, the equivalent then of about seventy-five thousand dollars. Her plans were correspondingly grandiose. There was some desirable property in Feldbach, not far from Zurich. The only catch was that the railroad would have to be relocated. Edith Rockefeller, whose father had slipped entire railroad companies into his pocket, saw this as no great hindrance. It took considerable diplomacy to convince her that one simply couldn't play with the Swiss National Railway as if it were the Baltimore and Ohio. Reluctantly, she let herself be talked into renting for the time being an elegant villa surrounded by gardens until some real estate came up whose acquisition would not spur her to attempt buying half the Swiss government. She rented the house for 30,000 francs and gave the club 360,000 francs as a stock fund, the interest of which was to cover its operating expenses. For many years she also covered the operating deficit, which then amounted to about twenty thousand francs a year.

The founding ceremonies of the club on February 26, 1916, were attended by about forty people. Emma Jung was voted its president; Edith McCormick was elected to the board of directors and Toni Wolff to the lecture committee. Harold Fowler McCormick headed the entertainment committee. He was a very gregarious, popular man who, though he spoke practically no German, could make himself easily understood by everyone. He played excellent pool and ping pong, often spotting his opponents twenty points. And he had no peer in organizing social events and party games. These games were generally rather innocuous; very popular was one in which the player saw only an eye through a peephole and had to guess whose eye it was.

But the lectures were the club's main focus, and the high points were those given by Jung himself two or three times a year. There, for example, he first presented some of the basic concepts of his typology. Also among the early lecturers was Wolf-Ferrari, the German-Italian composer, whom Edith Rockefeller was supporting and had psychoanalyzed as well. Jung apparently believed in the law of apostolic succession and had induced Edith McCormick, like so many others analyzed by him, to herself work as an analyst. When Wolf-Ferrari entered a slump and ceased composing, Jung, always close at hand with practical measures, advised Edith to sever the composer's support. Jung believed afterwards that this drastic step had effected a miracle cure. In any case, Wolf-Ferrari resumed composing. It has also been rumored that out of similar didactic motives Jung made Edith McCormick suddenly withdraw her financial support from James Joyce in 1919. Jung was said to have been disturbed by reports of Joyce's heavy drinking. Edith McCormick had earlier tried to persuade Joyce to undergo analysis by Jung but ran up against the writer's stubborn refusal. This may have aroused Jung's resentment.

The Psychological Club, in which one could also room and board, faced its first crisis in the second year of its existence when Irma Oczeret, the club's actuary, and her husband, a Jungian therapist, suddenly left the club. Asked about the cause of this precipitous withdrawal, Jung indicated that they had been evicted. It appeared that Herr Oczeret had maintained "concrete relationships" with his female clients and had collected an entire harem. Toni Wolff was then chosen to fill Frau Oczeret's position in the club. Other charter members resigned from the club soon after its founding.

But the first major crisis for the club came in the early twenties at a gathering convened by Jung when Alphonse Maeder and Hans Trüb, club president at the time, openly attacked their mentor. They decried his unwillingness to sit still for any serious discussion. He would not stick to the point; if others disagreed with him, he would turn authoritarian, or he would simply employ his technique of bodily escape. As if to demonstrate the aptness of these reproaches before their very eyes, Jung rose suddenly, said, "Well, yes, I think I'll be going," and stalked out of the meeting room. This hasty withdrawal elicited from the usually mild Alphonse Maeder the sarcastic comment: "There you have it. When you try to take the bull by the horns, he simply takes off." In a show of solidarity Emma Jung and Toni Wolff left the hall with Jung.

This unusual incident meant a small palace revolt; practically speaking, the Jungs had abdicated from their own club. And in fact, they and Toni Wolff stayed away from club activities for several years, until the mid-twenties when Hans Trüb stepped down from his post as president and the entire governing body was replaced.

Harold McCormick returned to the United States shortly after the end of World War I. Although he was not exactly destitute, his private fortune was rather modest next to his wife's. His financial contributions to the club were likewise more discreet. Nevertheless, before he left he gave 5,000 francs to establish the club library and wrote a check for 50,000 francs to set up a "Scholarship Trust Fund" for Jungian psychology. This money was to enable those less well-to-do to study Jungian psychology and to undergo analysis. In 1948 at the founding of the Jung Institute (from an organizational perspective an offshoot of the club) this fund, grown in the meantime to about seventy thousand francs, was transferred from the club to the new institute.

Edith McCormick returned to the United States in 1921. Shortly afterward she and her husband were divorced. In 1922 he married the Polish singer Ganna Walska. He was married again toward the end of his life, this time to Adah Wilson, a nurse. In his old age he underwent a rejuvenation cure, having himself injected with monkey serum. The aging process was not arrested. He died in 1941 at the age of sixty-nine.

Even after her return to the United States Edith McCormick maintained an interest in the fate of the Psychological Club, listing herself as a member in *Who's Who*. She continued her financial support until the end of the twenties. By that time she had fallen into the hands of a Swiss architect, Edwin Krenn, who persuaded her to finance his magnificent project. His sights were set on constructing an entire futuristic city, to be called "Edithopolis." This project consumed a huge portion of the Rockefeller millions. Edith also gave large sums to less quixotic ventures like the Chicago Zoological Garden and the Chicago Civic Opera. When she died in 1932 around her sixtieth birthday, her fortune had dwindled.

It is ironic that the (by Rockefeller standards) modest gift that launched the Psychological Club may have been Edith Rockefeller's most consequential donation. The founding of the Jungian club meant the social embodiment of Jungian psychology, the genesis of a sect which evolved very slowly and quietly at first, and whose growth only now, after an incubation period of several decades, seems to be accelerating. If a number of signs are not misleading, Carl Jung may yet emerge as the prophet of a new "psychologized" religiosity attuned to the Age of Aquarius in a way that Freud and the crisis-ridden Christian churches are not. And it would be curious indeed if his canonization had been given a decisive push by a capricious American clubwoman with a few crumbs of the oil millions of John D. Rockefeller.

11

INTROVERT AND EXTROVERT—
THE UNBRIDGEABLE CHASM

At the time the Psychological Club, the first center for Jungian psychology, was founded, Jungian psychology did not yet exist. It was only after 1916 that Jung slowly began to formulate his own doctrine. He did this largely in a polemical way, by a fractious repudiation of large tracts of the Freudian system. But his strenuous attempts to disentangle himself only highlighted his continuing dependence on psychoanalysis. For a long time, it remained the implicit system of coordinates by which he navigated. Not by chance did Jung name his own doctrine "analytical psychology"—a title he had once proposed for the Freudian theories.

From the very first, Jung had swallowed more of psychoanalysis than he could stomach. After the break with his Viennese mentor, he began to disgorge large chunks of it. Freudian findings he had earlier pronounced "empirically certain" had now lost in his eyes both their empiricism and their certainty. In particular, he began to disparage Freud's theories about the nature of dreams, which he had at one time extolled. To impute deceptive intents to dreams and to hypothetical dream censors, as Freud did, struck the post-Freudian Jung as the height of anthropomorphic folly. He declared that dreams are "products of nature," and that nature does not indulge in falsehood or legerdemain.

While he was at it, Jung also began to reject Freud's way of conceptualizing the unconscious. The Freudian "id" seemed to him too crude and petty bourgeois, a bare storage and boiler room of the personality, dark and claustrophobic. With his dreams of vast cellars and richly furnished vaults, Jung needed a larger, more stately image of the nether regions of the psyche. His stylish promotion of the collective unconscious, a mythopoeic treasure house of archetypal images, exposed the id for the puny thing it was.

During the years of semi-psychosis, Jung had invented a sort of art therapy to cope with the volcanic eruptions of his unconscious. After the crisis was past, he tried to formulate theoretically what he had discovered intuitively. But these early attempts at theorizing did not get much beyond the labeling stage. Thus the synthetic faculty that integrates unconscious material into awareness was called by him "the transcendent function," the method of interpreting fantasy images by the recourse to mythology, "amplification." Jung believed that his way of staying close, and constantly returning, to the original imagery was superior to the fanciful meanderings of free association. But he was unaware of the drawbacks of his technique, of its solipsism, its failure to "realize" the impulses from the unconscious in direct dealings with people. Exorcism by means of art is at best a compromise, as much a flight from, as a confrontation with, immediate reality. And we have reason to believe that Jung used the storehouses of ancient mythology as his private catacombs, as a device to keep the external world at bay.

Jung's practical and theoretical efforts to come to terms with the realm of the unconscious were an intensely personal affair. The same is true—though less obviously so—with regard to the massive typology which occupied him for nearly a decade and first established his worldwide fame.

This ambitious work was a piece of self-therapy. It had the surreptitious aim of stylizing Jung's clash with Freud, of showing that the feud arose from the fatalities of inborn character and was therefore unavoidable and unresolvable. The leitmotiv of Jung's characterology was that the chasm between introverts and extroverts (as he called the opposite types) is unbridgeable, that these two types, even when appearing to share the same world, perceive this world differently; when seeming to use a common language, attach divergent meanings to it; and when trying to interpret their shades of meaning to each other find that they are untranslatable. The conflicts between the two types, according to Jung, are caused by prerational commitments so basic and ineluctable that attempts at compromise are fruitless. Their world views being incommensurable, the differences between them may be glossed over but cannot be reasoned away.

Jung's typology owed much to the work of the American philosopher William James. Although having little use for James's pragmatism, Jung eagerly adopted the American's notion that every philosophy is built on subjective premises and that the history of philosophy is largely the history of the clash of human *temperaments*. The true philosopher, James wrote, tries to think the facts of his temperament. "Yet his temperament gives him a stronger bias than any of his more strictly objective premises . . . in the forum he can make no claim, on the bare ground of his temperament, to superior discernment or authority. There arises thus a certain insincerity in our philosophic discussions, the potentest of all our premises is never mentioned." James distinguishes two basic types, the "tough-minded" and the "tender-minded." The former, he says, are "empiricists," lovers of "facts in all their crude variety." The tender-minded, on the other hand, are "rationalists" or "idealists," devotees of "abstract and eternal principles." The antagonism between these two types, whenever "their temperaments have been intense, has formed in all ages a part of the philosophic atmosphere of the time. It forms a part of the atmosphere today. The tough think of the tender as sentimentalists and soft-heads. The tender feel the tough to be unrefined, callous, or brutal. . . . Each type believes the other to be inferior to itself." By stressing the crucial role of the subjective factor in philosophy, James made it difficult for later philosophers to assert their objectivity in good faith.

Emulating James, Jung used typology to undermine the absolute claims of established orthodoxies. With the help of his typological theory of relativity (and extending his typology from persons to theoretical systems), Jung declared psychoanalysis to be an extroverted doctrine, one-sidedly oriented toward the external world and viewing this world as the ultimate touchstone of reality.[1] For a while, Jung thought of his own

[1]However, Freud, the originator of this "extroverted" system, was diagnosed by Jung as an introvert. In Jung's view, psychoanalysis was "the expression of the unlived (repressed) extroversion of Freud."

psychology as the (introverted) opposite of psychoanalysis, but eventually decided to assign this position to Alfred Adler's school. This proved to be a stroke of genius, making Jung's doctrine the superior mediator between the "extremist," and hence strictly limited, views of Adler and Freud. Already in 1913, Jung had suggested that "the most difficult task of the future" would be "to create a psychology that does equal justice to both types." Even then it was easy to guess whom he had in mind as the architect of this synthesis.

Psychological Types was first published in 1921. Over five hundred pages long, the book displayed the painstaking and pedantic thoroughness of the Germanic scholar; with its mania for footnotes, citations, and references, it exhausts the reader as much as the topic under discussion. Despite its show of erudition, *Psychological Types* was not a very profound or original work. Its success may be attributed, in fact, to its combination of massive scholarship with a certain shallowness of thought. It provides the reader with handy typological labels that can be used without much mental strain to impose a semblance of order on a vast body of factual material. For those who mistake mere labeling for genuine psychological understanding, there are some facile typological formulas, easily memorized, easily associated with the name of Jung, and hence serviceable as labels for Jung's doctrine itself, though they hardly touch its core.

Jung's typology could draw on an immense body of earlier work. From time immemorial, amateur and professional psychologists have relished drawing up more or less elaborate typologies promising cheap insight into—and power over—their fellows. There is no end to this sort of invention. Schemes of character have been innumerable—from Galen's four temperaments (sanguine, phlegmatic, choleric, and melancholic) which dominated Western characterology for centuries, to fairly recent attempts, like those of Sheldon, to establish empirical correlations between character and body build. When the basic types are sketched with a quasi-artistic intuition—as, for instance, with Ernst Kretschmer's "pyknics" and "asthenics"—such schemes have the power to fascinate the reader. As long as we remain under their spell, we are compelled, as it were, to view the people we meet through their lenses. Yet the insight gained in this way is at the cost of our acuteness to individual nuances.

The fact that typologies are manufactured in endless succession is a sure sign that they promise much more than they deliver. They are easy to come by, but that very ease proclaims their futility. What the German physicist Georg Lichtenberg said about physiognomics over two hundred years ago holds true for typology today: "I have always found that people of mediocre knowledge of the world expected most from systematic physiognomics. Men who know the world are the best physiognomists and expect least from general rules."

Jung did not stint his efforts in working out his own typology, but in the end he did not get much further than his predecessors. He began with a simplistic scheme containing only two basic categories: "introversion," designating a "thinking type" who abstracts from objects; and "extroversion," referring to a "feeling type," who gropes his way into objects. Jung realized soon that this crude scheme was untenable. It simply would not do to equate introversion, which designated a *direction* (away from the object) more than anything else, with the function of thinking, and to amalgamate extroversion with feeling. As was his wont, Jung gradually elaborated and complicated his scheme until, in its final eightfold form, it became more convoluted than most previous typologies.

Eventually, Jung added a classification based on specific psychic functions to his original scheme.[2] Each "function type," defined in terms of his dominant function, could be either introverted or extroverted. This revised scheme, generating eight distinct types, was further complicated by Jung's attempts to account for the person's "unconscious character." Every human being, he asserted, has the potential for all of the basic modes. The conscious introvert is an unconscious extrovert, and vice versa. A thinking type (whether extrovert or introvert) whose feeling function seems totally atrophied has not actually forfeited his emotionality. However stunted, it retains the impulse to assert itself, to emerge into awareness. It is true that the early disenfranchisement of certain modes is part of the process of normal psychic development. It is equally true, however, that this process often reverses itself in later life: the "pure intellect" may be pushed by his one-sidedness into an impasse, forcing the development of his feeling side. If the early repression has been severe, and the deconstriction sudden, the breakthrough of the latent type will be explosive: a mutation of the personality seems to occur. But transitions from one function type to another may also be smooth. In fact, the Jungian analyst, using Jung's typology as a road map, aims to bring about a gentle unfolding of the shriveled functions. Jung believed, in his own case, that the intuitive faculty he had spurned over the years gradually surfaced in middle age, contesting the supremacy of rational thinking, up-to-then his dominant function.

From an objective point of view, Jung's typology has serious flaws. Thus, the introvert–extrovert dichotomy is overly coarse and forces independent factors—such as social behavior (outgoing or withdrawing) and emotional reactivity (thin-skinned

[2]The four basic functions identified by Jung are: sensation, thinking, feeling, and intuition.

or thick-skinned)—into the same ill-fitting pigeonhole. As to the four basic functions, their choice and delineation seem arbitrary. Why are there exactly four of them, and why precisely those four? Jung does not tell. It is questionable whether intuition is "basic" in the Jungian sense. And if intuition, why not also imagination and memory? And what does Jung gain by the "disembodied" nature of his typology, its lack of interest in the physical concomitants of character, its disregard of the basic category of "temperament"? The reasons Jung gives for these omissions are far from convincing. Finally, what are we to make of the relative neglect of the dynamic aspects of the personality, of energy level, drive, need, impulsivity, and so forth? It is baffling to see these factors relegated to second rank by a psychologist who, in other contexts, is quite preoccupied with the energetics of the psyche.

However peculiar some of the premises of Jung's typology, they can be directly derived from the idiosyncrasies of its creator. Why there must be exactly four basic functions is hardly justified by Jung's argument that he had simply determined an empirical fact. But given his reverence for the number four as the quintessence of perfection, it is not surprising that his scheme was fourfold. Similarly, the choice of intuition as one of the basic functions may be understood as expressing a personal proclivity: to Carl Jung, the visionary, a highly developed intuition was the most vital organ of perception.

Jung's description of introversion and extroversion also constitutes a special plea. In Jung's era psychoanalysis, and Western civilization in general, favored the extrovert at the expense of the introvert, tending to view the former as "healthy" and the latter as "neurotic." Jung tried to redress the balance by stressing that the introvert's search for the "kingdom within" was just as legitimate as the extrovert's fascination with the external world. This rehabilitation of subjectivity is most welcome to those admittedly few and unfashionable psychologists who—unlike the behavioristic types dominating American psychology—have not entirely lost sight of the inner world of the psyche. Such unseasonable psychologists will insist, even at the risk of being ridiculed, that, in the end, it is the *endo*psychic sector, which Jung called the *soul,* that judges without further appeal the ultimate value and meaning of all that befalls us from without.

Again and again in his typology, Jung stops to emphasize that our overall relationship to the world precedes any rational judgment, and that, given their diametrically opposed starting positions, misunderstandings between the various types are inevitable. "The introvert can never wholly comprehend the extravert," the anthropologist Edward Sapir wrote in a review of *Psychological Types,* "because he cannot resign himself to what he inevitably feels to be a vicarious existence. To him the extravert must ever seem a little superficial, a chronic vagrant from the spirit's home. Nor can the extravert wholly convince himself that behind the introvert's reserve and apparent impoverishment of interest there may lie the greatest wealth of experience, and such subtlety of feeling as he may hardly parallel in his own external responses." Reading between Jung's lines, one senses that he claimed for himself the "subtlety of feeling" not always apparent in his external responses. He also seems to have used his thesis of irredeemable differences among opposite types to exonerate himself from the guilt caused by his falling-out with Freud.

In general, Jung's typology can be viewed as an episode of his continuing effort to free himself from the Viennese master.

C. G. Jung—The Haunted Prophet

By advancing a sort of psychological theory of relativity, Jung also undermined psychoanalytic claims to absolute validity. Since its first aim is to constrict the authority of a formidable opponent, we immediately suspect that this relativism is only provisional, and that behind it, hidden to our view, the absolutism of a new orthodoxy is taking shape. The further course of Jung's life will amply confirm this suspicion. To be sure, during this and later periods, Jung pays much lip-service to the existence of limits on the validity of his own theory. But these ritual disclaimers convince only those who do not *want* to see the dogmatism permeating the work of Carl Jung.

12

JUNG
IN AMERICA

Early in 1920 Jung completed his *Psychological Types*. The
next five or six years were a period of consolidation. They were
also a period of travel when Jung made major expeditions to
North Africa (Tunis and Algeria), East Africa (Kenya and
Uganda), and North America (where he studied the Pueblo
Indians of the Southwest). These journeys were—how could it
be otherwise with Jung?—not merely geographical voyages;
they were deeply symbolic attempts to approach the unconscious from the outside, as it were, historically and "geologi-
cally." Jung was hoping somehow to discover that layers of the
psyche buried deep in the unconscious of civilized Westerners
were still near the surface of consciousness with so-called primitive, archaic tribes. While this was an anthropological fallacy,
it was one not uncommon in those days.

C. G. Jung—The Haunted Prophet

During the same period when Jung was traveling through widely scattered areas, he was also sinking his roots more deeply into his native soil. In 1922 he bought land in Bollingen on upper Lake Zurich, and in 1923 he began to build the tower which for the rest of his life would be his retreat and resting place. He continued to expand it nearly to the end of his days. It was *his* house, much more so than his family residence in Küsnacht, and increasingly it became the symbol in stone of his own personality. Jung said that he built the tower "in a sort of dream." Begun shortly after his mother's death in 1923, the work was not completed until thirty-three years later, one year after the death of his wife. After she died, Jung, already eighty years old, said he felt the inner obligation to finally assume his own self. This meant that he was able at last to finish his tower, enlarging the till-then stunted middle part of his organically evolved retreat. With the completion of this building, Jung indicated, the unfolding of his self as well was essentially complete.

In the end it was his cloisterlike tower existence in Bollingen, where he shunned electricity and the telephone to connect more easily with an age-old chain of being, that expressed Jung's life-style most clearly. But in the early 1920s, when his tower was first a plan and then only an embryonic reality, he broadened the reach of his experience through his great and far-reaching expeditions.

The theme of Jung's field trips was "Away from Europe," geographically and culturally, away from Europe's overwrought civilization with its hyperconsciousness, its tame domesticity, its repressed emotions, and its breathless pace. Jung wanted to find an Archimedean footing from which to render visible the buried premises, the foregone conclusions, and the constrictions of Europe's world view. His journeys to Africa and the

American Southwest were attempts to rediscover in the outer world the archaic and pregnant riches he had found during his explorations within. And as during his submersion in his own depths he was aware of the lurking danger of psychosis, so in his journeys to the dark continent he felt threatened by the danger of "going black under the skin," of being overwhelmed by the intensity of life in an alien environment. To an eye schooled by Jung it appears anything but chance or mere physical accident that on all of these trips Jung succumbed to serious illnesses and infections and that the eventual ruin of his health dates back to the amoebic dysentery he contracted in India in 1938 on the last of his journeys to exotic regions.

On the first of his trips to Africa Jung stayed on the periphery of the black continent, close to Europe. But even this first journey to a milieu outside Europe (not counting his earlier trips to the USA), in which the "white man" was an alien intruder, brought Jung an abundance of intense and enduring experiences. "This Africa is unheard of," began a letter to Emma Jung from the Grand Hotel in Sousse, in which, with a fine gift for observation, and with swift impressionistic strokes of the pen, he described the enormous wealth of color, the swirl of people, costumes, and architecture, the magical flora and fauna of the tropics, noting also that the guttural cries of the burnoose vendors could very well come from the canton of Zurich. "This is only miserable stammering," he wrote closing a letter that was anything but mere stammers. "I don't know quite what Africa says to me, but it is speaking. Imagine a mighty sun, air as clear as on the highest mountains, a sea bluer than you have ever seen, every color of unheard-of strength, in the market you can still buy the amphora of antiquity, such a thing—and the moon! . . ."

Jung's intensity of perception was heightened through his

contact with the Moorish soil to the point that a kind of olfactory hallucination befell him there: the land smelled peculiar to him, it smelled of blood, as though the earth itself were bloodsoaked. The feverish excitement he sensed behind the mask of Oriental apathy possessed him. He would sit for hours in Arab coffee houses watching the play of expressions across faces and eavesdropping on conversations of which he understood not a word. He registered no particular shock at the open and commonplace homosexuality.

Jung felt he had been placed in a naive world of adolescents threatened with destruction by the poison of Western civilization. His own European obsession with the clock, the chopping up of time into hours, minutes, seconds, gradually sank away as in a dream. The deeper he pushed into the inner country the more his time slowed, crept to a standstill, even oddly reversed itself. He found his surmise borne out that the apathy of these people was only a mask when he saw it give way to intense excitement at festivals and collective work efforts. He concluded that these people, unlike Europeans, lived directly from their emotions, "rather, they are lived by them."

Jung felt "psychically infected" and experienced his inner excitement as a threat. He felt himself transported back into a not-so-safe childhood paradise. After a few weeks there the Arab world that had been so exotic at first glance seemed to him an ancient memory of a forgotten and all too familiar past. "It is the memory of a still extant way of life which, however, has been overgrown by civilization. Were we to naively re-experience it, it would be a reversion to barbarity." As so often with Jung, he first became aware of being endangered through impressive dreams of warning. In one such dream he found himself entangled in a life-and-death wrestling match with a handsome young Arab, a youth of royal bearing. After overcoming his opponent, Jung forced him "with fatherly kindness" to read a book Jung had written—a heavy fine for losing an erotically tinged wrestling match!

Jung interpreted the dream as ominous. To him, the life-and-death struggle with the Arab youth meant that his identity was threatened, that he was near the point of being overpowered by the North African world and dragged by it into the dark whirlpool of the unconscious. An unrealized potential of his seemed to be embodied in the way of life of the dark kingly youth, and Jung fled the temptation to live out this "shadow" part by returning to Europe.

But he was "psychically infected" by Africa in more than one way. He felt that he simply had to go back again, had to push deeper into the interior of this mysterious, alluring continent—the setting of *She*, one of his favorite novels. He was compelled to wait five years before he could realize this wish.

In the fall of 1925 Jung had an opportunity to make a second voyage to Africa. This time he traveled with two friends, one English and one American, from London via Genoa and Port Said to Mombassa in East Africa, and from there to Nairobi. On the trip from Mombassa to Nairobi Jung was overcome with a sense of *déjà vu*, as though centuries ago he had been familiar with the exotic figures and landscapes of East Africa. This mood stayed with him throughout the entire five months he was to spend on the dark continent. As earlier in North Africa, Jung fancied himself in a dream state, though his powers of perception were sharp.

From Nairobi the three friends traveled to Kakamega, the seat of a British District Commissioner, where they recruited a forty-eight–man support column and a three-man armed

C. G. Jung—The Haunted Prophet

escort (more symbolically than militarily effective), and then marched for five days to the foot of Mt. Elgon, an inactive volcano 4,400 meters high. This was essentially the goal of the journey. They established camp halfway up the mountain in a wide clearing not far from an Elgonyi village. On the way from Nairobi to Mt. Elgon the three white men had been joined by an Englishwoman who shared their itinerary. Jung was pleased with this arrangement. He saw in it the subtle workings of archetypal forces that, according to his views, seek to transform every triad into the more perfect form of the quaternity.

The expedition was not without its adventures, in the guise of hungry hyenas, poisonous snakes, and excitable Africans. But Jung felt in his element. Europe, "the mother of all demons," was far away; no phone calls or telegrams could disrupt his "divine peace." He was acutely aware that he was experiencing this other-worldly peace just before the end came. Soon even this still-unspoiled region would be overrun by the machine-ridden civilization of the white man.

As always, Jung inquired about the religious ideas and the dreams of the native people around him. With his pidgin-Swahili and the aid of a lexicon, he could make himself tolerably understood by the Elgonyi. So he organized regular palavers over which he presided on a small mahogany chief's stool. To his dismay, however, he could learn virtually nothing of the dreams of the Elgonyi. When Jung asked the old Laibon, the medicine man, about his dreams, the old man tearfully explained that in earlier times the Laibon had had many dreams of guidance and prophesy, but since the advent of the white man these dream visions had vanished; apparently they were no longer needed, since the English knew everything anyway. Jung was shaken by this disclosure. It confirmed his fear that

African culture would disintegrate. The resignation of the Elgonyi Laibon reminded him of accounts of the Papuans of New Guinea who, after the British arrived, came to believe that even the crocodiles had turned their loyalty over to the colonial lords out of an instinctive recognition of the true power situation. This was borne out for them when a convict who had escaped from British authorities was terribly mangled by a crocodile while trying to cross a river. Evidently the animal had become a police-crocodile in the service of the white rulers.

Jung was at first able to learn little about the religion, rites, and ceremonies of the Elgonyi. Direct questioning yielded few results. These people seemed reluctant to talk about religious topics. They also found it difficult to associate anything concrete with abstract concepts like religion and religious ceremonies. So Jung had to rely mostly on his own observations.

In this way he came to conclude that the Elgonyi identified very directly with the plant and animal life of their world Because of this "participation mystique" with living nature it did not occur to them to set themselves above the "other animals." Insofar as they acknowledged a hierarchy within the animal kingdom, they assigned the highest rung not to "Homo sapiens" but to the far more majestic elephant. Even the mighty lion, the python, and the crocodile were valued as more important than the two-legged creature who must take great pains merely to preserve his life from the caprices of these powerful beasts.

Jung observed also that the realm of imagination in the Elgonyi was split into two worlds of day and night, as distinctly separate from each other as the African day and the African night. By day, their world was defined by the sunshine of a pure, unconquerable optimism. In this perspective even sickness and death could be easily accepted. A man takes sick, and he dies; that is all there is to it. No one has a lot of stupid notions about what might happen after death. He simply does not breathe anymore. His body is taken to the bush where the hyenas will eat it. With that, the whole affair is over, settled. By day. But with the sudden descent of the equatorial night, the whole nature of their imagination changed abruptly. The world is now ruled by evil powers, by the spirits of the dead; man and beast are threatened with pestilence; the night wanderer is attacked; and other acts of terror are committed. One tries to protect himself against these dangers with magic practices. The Elgonyi were not conscious of the contradictory nature of these two attitudes. They seemed as little concerned about this discrepancy as the average Westerner is about the contrast between the white magic of his technology and the black or gray magic of his own cult ceremonies.

Jung's stay with the Elgonyi was blissful for him. He was reluctant to leave on the appointed day of departure. He firmly promised himself that he would return to this blessed country. When he did so ten years later, he found no longer the land of his dreams. Goldfields around Mt. Elgon had drastically altered the face of the landscape and the life of the people. Jung was right in his melancholy premonition that he had experienced this ancient world in its untouched beauty and deep passion as it was ending forever.

On the return trip, which led across the Sudan and then up the Nile to Khartoum, Jung tried to clarify the abundance of his African experiences. As he reviewed the dreams he had had on this journey, it occurred to him that they dealt only with Europeans and scenes of his homeland and appeared to stubbornly ignore Africa. Only once during those six months had he dreamed of a Negro, and that was a barber who had given him a shave and haircut in Chattanooga, Tennessee. In this dream, the black man held a gigantic red-hot curling-iron to Jung's head and wanted to make his hair kinky! Before the barber succeeded in this endeavor Jung awoke, terrified. He took this as another warning of the ever-present danger of "going black," of being swallowed up by his unconscious. The fact that the dream employed a twelve-year-old memory of an American Negro indicated to Jung that the impact of his African experiences was being softened by his unconscious.

It gradually dawned on Jung during his homeward journey out of the "wilds of Africa" that this expedition had been mostly symbolic and symptomatic and not, as he had first imagined, a simple ethnological field trip. He now saw that it was closely tied to his own burning personal problems. It was part flight (from his family and Toni Wolff), part another form of the midnight journey, a new attempt to delve into the alluring and abysmal world of the unconscious, to make it visible in the light of consciousness, and thus to tame its demonic power.

***

Since the earliest days of his intellectual life Jung had been fascinated by the riddle of the American mentality and the American destiny. Even in the first years of his psychiatric practice there were a great many Americans among his patients. Jung often compared himself laughingly with an Indian medicine man whose prestige is greater the greater his geographical distance from the cure-seekers. He was struck by how radically the mentality of relatively new Americans differed from that of their European forebears, from whom they were

C. G. Jung—The Haunted Prophet

separated by only one or two generations. On the basis of his experiences with American patients he arrived at astounding generalizations about Americans. He determined, for example, that all Americans suffered from an enormous mother complex which manifested itself in their puritanical attitudes toward sex.[1] He noted very early the "feminization" of the American male and the "masculinization" of the American woman; with a keen eye he described the symptoms of "Momism" long before Philip Wylie (who, by the way, based himself on Jung); and with great acuteness he recognized the insufferable position of the American woman, psychologically overelevated and socially disenfranchised. He predicted the advent of a radical American women's movement long before it became a social reality.

Jung was remarkably free of the usual arrogance of the European intellectual toward everything American. He approached the USA far more receptively and impartially than Freud and decided very early that nothing could be more useful for Europeans than to take a look at Europe from the top of an American skyscraper.

Long before it became a platitude of European journalists in the late 1940s Jung saw between the USA and the USSR, in spite of their opposed ideologies (which he himself took very seriously), subterranean, geopolitical, and social convergences. He saw for the two continents a common destiny, dictated by the wide open spaces of these giant land masses containing giant nations, and he saw Europe threatened by the twin dan-

[1]In 1942, Jung told the Swiss historian Carl Burckhardt that Franklin D. Roosevelt, the "limping messenger of the apocalypse," had "of course, like all Americans, a gigantic mother complex." Like all people suffering from such a complex, Jung held, Roosevelt tried to please his mother by being an idealist, and, at the same time, to enchant the woman in her by being a super-rascal.

gers of Bolshevization and Americanization. He was aware that the Americanization of the European upper classes had already made great strides long before America's cultural invasion of Europe in the wake of World War II. However, while he detested Bolshevism with his whole being as an areligious ideology that dwarfed man into an amorphous mass being, Jung regarded the "American way of life" quite positively. (His fanatical hatred of Bolshevism, in combination with his religious "spiritualism," may have been one reason for his popularity in certain American circles; this anti-Bolshevism also may have led him initially to welcome the Nazi "revolution," whose profound nihilism dawned on him relatively late.)

In any case, it was clear to Jung that the follies and excesses of American life, so often ridiculed by Europeans, soon lost this ridiculous quality if one experienced the culture as a totality from the inside, with an understanding of its ethos, its aspirations, and its unavoidable limitations.

What particularly fascinated Jung was the apparent "mutation" of spirit, character, and even physiognomy which the transplanting of European settlers into American soil seemed to have effected in an incredibly short time.[2] In his efforts to explain this, Jung emphasized the particular circumstances of American history: these settlers of European origin had invaded the continent as conquerors and, like his friend Graf Keyserling, Jung held that the conquerors of foreign lands "take their bodies with them, certainly, but not their souls."

Jung saw the collective soul of America as largely deter-

[2]Noteworthy differences existed in the psychic dispositions of European and American patients who perhaps still had a common grandfather. These differences went much deeper than the superficial variations in content one would naturally expect with relocation to a new environment.

mined by Indian and Negro influences. Even before his first trip to America he had observed the huge role played by the black and the red man in the unconscious of his American patients. In dreams the black man regularly embodied the "shadow," the unlived life-potential, while the red man symbolized the Ego-ideal, the idealistic aspiration of Americans. When he did come to America, Jung saw in the social behavior of countless Americans—with their incessant chatter (including the printed gabble of newspapers with their glib gossip columns), their body movements both careless and charged with energy, their unrestrained guffawing laughter, and (for a European) unheard-of gregariousness and public quality of their existence—a striking resemblance to the mode of life of Central African Negro villages. Without knowing it, these people were in their total conduct deeply affected by their former slaves. (Jung, by the way, did not place a negative value on this "Negro-ization" of America.)

But far deeper and more unconscious, according to Jung, was the psychic imprint of the Indian upon Americans. It went so deep as to visibly mark their physical body. On his first trip to the USA Jung saw American workers in Buffalo streaming out of a factory after work; he wondered at the distinctly Indian character of many of their faces and remarked to an American companion that he had not realized that so much Indian blood flowed in the veins of white Americans. His companion replied, laughing, that he would be willing to bet there was not one drop of Indian blood to be found in these hundreds of men. This made the whole affair much more mysterious for Jung. Shortly thereafter he discovered that the American anthropologist Boas had observed typical anatomical changes already in second-generation Americans, particularly in the dimensions of the skull.[3]

Even as he reflected on Flournoy's American patient called "Miss Miller," whose fantasies provided the raw material for his *Transformations and Symbols of the Libido*, Jung was astounded at how great a role the Hiawatha-mythos played in her fantasies. Jung made similar observations with his own American patients. Thus the actual red man, who had been victimized by the white invaders, was generally idealized in the unconscious of whites, whereas the black man, representing the shunned shadow, was distorted into a demonic figure. So when the chance came in 1924 for a field trip to the Pueblo Indians, Jung took it. Now he would be able to observe close at hand the living models of those fantasy images he had encountered so often.

Since the language barrier was less formidable than it had been in Africa, Jung managed to parley quite well with some of the Indians, in particular with Ochwiay Biano (Mountain Lake), a chief of the Taos Pueblos. Jung was charmed and deeply moved that he could converse with this "primitive" from an entirely different culture and could come to speak quite naturally of things, and more honestly than he could with most Europeans. (Many of the Pueblo chief's remarks which Jung wrote down sound like an anticipation of the teachings of Castaneda's Don Juan.)

Jung was most anxious to learn as much as he could about the religious attitudes of the Pueblo Indians. First of all he discovered that for outsiders their religion was concealed behind a thick veil of mystery. But this involved not the secret

[3]Boas's findings are disputed today.

of one single priest, nor the secret of a small elite, but rather a sacred mystery shared by the entire tribe through which it kept its unity before the outer world. Jung, who had intuitively linked mystery and religion since his earliest youth, was pleased to find his presentiment confirmed; but thanks to his friendship with Ochwiay Biano he succeeded in gaining partial access to the carefully guarded secret. To be sure, the way of direct questioning was excluded. Only by sensitive, careful indirection was Jung able to come by a little knowledge of the Pueblo religion.

Jung was struck by the Indians' solemnity in matters of religion. The otherwise serene and impassive Indian fell into a visible flutter of emotion as soon as he began to speak about religious themes. His religion centered on the sun, to him the visible godhead and father of all that lives. Jung's careful question, whether one might not imagine the sun as the creation of an invisible god, appeared simply absurd to Ochwiay. He replied, categorically, "The sun is God. Everyone can see that."

The core of the Pueblo religion was that the deity sun needed the assistance of his sons, the Pueblos, who lived on the roof of the world. Their religious practices helped the Sunfather through his daily course. They believed that if their religion were to die out the sun would die, too, and the world be left in eternal night. As sons of the sun, the meaning of life and their cosmological worth were secure for the Pueblos. Jung, as a religiously uprooted European, could not resist envying their obvious cosmic security. He acknowledged this religious envy and the spiritual impoverishment of most contemporary Europeans without smirking defensively at the "naivete" of the Indians. And he found some solace in the thought that the central idea of the Pueblo religion—that God requires the cooperation of his creatures to carry out and perfect His existence—had long been familiar to him through the writings of medieval Christian mystics like Meister Eckhart and through his own meditations on the mystery of the God-Father-Son relationship.

After his stay with the Pueblo Indians, Jung was even more convinced than before of the profound imprint of the American Indian upon the collective mind of America. Jung noted that Americans were obsessed, to an unusual degree, by the pursuit of a sort of Heroic Ideal, and that this heroic attitude, with its primitive reckless features, had been largely acquired through identification with the Red Man. Jung cited American sports, the "toughest" in the world, from which the idea of play had almost disappeared, as a prime example of this heroic stance. He stressed the parallels between the initiation ceremonies of American college fraternities and those of Indian tribes. He was struck by the profusion of secret societies of every description, from the Ku Klux Klan to the Knights of Columbus, and by the resemblance of their rites to those of primitive mystery religions. And he did not fail to notice the analogy between the spiritual healing of Christian Science and the shamanistic practices of American Indians, observing that both, though unscientific, proved to be "pretty effective." He saw this "Indianization" of the American mind even tangibly mirrored in the skyline of New York or Chicago, with the "houses piling up to towers towards the centre," just like the pueblos of the southwestern Indians. "Without conscious imitation the American unconsciously fills out the spectral outline of the Red Man's mind and temperament."

Jung kept returning to what he viewed as the crux of the

C. G. Jung—The Haunted Prophet

American dilemma. The national prejudice of Americans, he wrote, is to be as harmless as possible or to view themselves as such; charged with the "unpleasant task of having to digest primitive peoples," the American must believe in himself to the utmost, in order to escape psychic disintegration. Hence, according to Jung, Americans as a nation are apt to believe in the purity of their motives and to be abysmally blind vis-à-vis their darker instincts.

Regarding America's role on the world stage, Jung was extremely ambivalent. After World War II, he expressed alarm at the growing cultural ascendancy of the United States, which he saw as promoting the rule of "mass man" and of the "mass psyche." To a correspondent in Chile he wrote in 1947: ". . . mass man breeds mass catastrophe. The greatest dangers today are the huge mass States like Russia and America." Jung tried to console himself and his correspondent by adding that, according to the lessons of history, such monster states are usually short-lived.

But when in 1949 a prominent American, Dorothy Thompson,[4] asked Jung in a letter for his opinion concerning the political role of America and its dealings with Soviet Russia, Jung professed himself a strong proponent of American hegemony. In the face of what he saw as the Russian threat, he held that Europe ought to be "organized by the U.S.A. *à tort et à travers* if need be." He was certain, he wrote, that Russia was "on the warpath" and that only the fear of those "in the know" was restraining her. But Jung warned against a military attack on Russia: "Russia can only defeat herself."

[4] In the 1920s Dorothy Thompson had told Edmund Wilson that the author Alexander Woollcott had gone to Jung for psychoanalysis and that what this revealed was that Woollcott was in love with Harpo Marx.

Viewing, as was his wont, the situation in psychological terms, Jung stated that any attempt to destroy "the enemy"—i.e., Russia—by force would be self-destructive, "since Russia is, as it were, identical with our unconscious, which contains our instincts and all the germs of future development." Once we in the West understood about "Russia inside ourselves," we would know how to deal with Russia politically.

America and its Western allies seemed to Jung politically vulnerable because of their spiritual crisis. He saw as a major symptom of this crisis the increasing emphasis on "social welfare." Jung for himself preferred "a modest poverty or any tangible discomfort (e.g., no bathroom, no electricity, no car, etc.)" to the train of neuroses, divorces, and other psychological "pests" he viewed as the direct results of social meliorism. The police terror in Russia and Nazi Germany was, in Jung's eyes, an "inevitable consequence" of those countries' attempts to institute "social welfare." "Why not 'spiritual welfare'?" Jung asked rhetorically, and scored the indifference of the governments of the earth to their citizens' psychological well-being.

That Jung was, by and large, pro-American may have been not unrelated to the largesse he repeatedly experienced from American millionaires. But while he was fond of the American upper class, Jung was rather critical of most American intellectuals and academics. He often deplored their superficiality and their lack of thorough grounding in the classics—a lack which in his eyes disqualified them as truly educated men. When the American psychology professor Calvin Hall sent Jung the draft of a chapter on Jungian psychology, Jung accused Hall of not knowing what he was talking about. He wrote Hall that a European who was about to write a treatise on, say, Plato's

C. G. Jung—The Haunted Prophet

philosophical works would feel duty-bound to read *all* the writings of Plato, and not less than half. An author who neglected to study the complete body of Plato's work would hardly be considered responsible or reliable. And not even with respect to such "an unimportant" figure as Jung himself was such remissness advisable.

Jung was particularly incensed that Hall had called him an occultist. He replied that if his study of religious, mythological, and folklorist fantasies earned him such a title, then Freud, because of his investigation of sexual fantasies, ought to be labeled a sexual pervert. Jung added that he failed to understand why Hall and others viewed the study of sexual fantasies as more "scientific" than the exploration of religious ideas. He accused Hall of ignoring the *facts* upon which Jungian psychology was based.

When a few years later another American psychologist, Richard I. Evans of the University of Houston, interviewed Jung, the latter was even more acerbic about the intellectual shoddiness of this American interlocutor. In a letter to a B.B.C. official, Jung called Evans a "professor of psychology who did not know anything and with whom an intelligent conversation was not possible." Jung added that at the time of the Evans interviews he still felt strong enough to push aside this untaught interviewer and to speak quite freely about some basic concepts of his psychology. But he was weary of repetitions of this sort of venture.

Despite his mishaps with these and other American academics, Jung was all in all rather pleased by the reception of his work in the United States. He was not unaware of the fact that his books were more widely read there than in Europe and that he was more of a prophet in that faraway land than in his own country. And his recognition by Americans may have been one of the reasons that Jung, in spite of many misgivings, always had a tender spot for America.

13

ALCHEMY—THE MAGIC SCIENCE

The Jung who returned so reluctantly from East Africa to the confines of Switzerland in 1926 was a changed man. Some of Africa's sun had burned its way into his soul. From then on he would face Europe from an ironic distance. "Europe is a jam-packed peninsula and not a continent," he wrote to his friend Graf Keyserling. "Everyone is jealous of his little place in the sun; the European is essentially petty." These and similar plaints about the "cradle of all devils" were to recur constantly in his writings.

After his return to his native land, Jung put more and more of his life into his "Tower Existence" at Bollingen. Long periods of solitude became a necessity for him. He complained that the twentieth century lacked secular cloisters where those weary of the empty bustle of daily life could "live outside of time." He longed to recapture the "blissful" existence granted him in his tent in the African wilderness. (Jung yearned all his life for the mothering darkness and safety of a cloistered place. With the shortage of fuel during World War II as an excuse, he built himself a dark wooden enclosure around the fireplace in his living room at Küsnacht, allegedly to save on heat. This little indoor tent project was not much of a hit with his family.)

The Jung of 1926 had not yet found his own path. For eight years, since 1918, he had been delving into the writings of the Hellenistic Gnostics and Neoplatonists. On the whole, these texts, though rich, proved disappointing. They were part of a lost, radically different culture. Only through tortuous mental acrobatics could they be related to twentieth-century thought. Jung's forays into old Chinese and Indian philosophy also led to dead ends. They made him realize that the spiritual malaise of modern Europe could only be cured by spiritual forces rooted in Europe's own tradition and not by an infusion of imported cultural goods. "What good is the wisdom of the Upanishads to us, or the insights of Chinese yoga," he asked, "if we forsake our own foundations . . . and settle thievishly on foreign shores like homeless pirates?" The more widely he ranged intellectually, the more he kept returning to the same theme: the greedy swallowing of spiritual gems and curios from all over the world, snatched from their contexts, instead of stilling the European's—and American's—spiritual hunger, was bound to give him indigestion. Only the most strenuous efforts of assimilation could open whatever healing potential these exotic cultures might possess.

Jung's own efforts at assimilation were frustrated at the time. And he also was beginning to find his analytic work increasingly frustrating. Having surmounted his spiritual crisis, he was less anxious than before to deal with the dilemmas of others. He started to resent the vampirism of his patients. "Therapy consumes," he was to write in old age. Even then he was grumbling that his patients were "eating [him] up," and that his resistances against these civilized cannibals were "gathering like storm clouds." To an American who inquired about psychotherapy with schizophrenics Jung replied that he had analyzed only a few cases of *acute* schizophrenia and that whenever possible he avoided handling such patients. While one could sometimes treat them successfully, this success "practically costs one one's life." The therapist had to make a superhuman effort, Jung felt, to glue the splintered fragments of the schizophrenic psyche back together.

Thus it was a disgruntled, sullen Jung, forever seeking and increasingly restive, who returned from the paradise of East Africa to his Swiss homeland. The homecoming was to him a sort of exile as well; just such a Swiss village, he confessed in his old age, he had often dreamed of stamping into the ground. But, as had happened to him before in similar impasses, a providential convergence of inner and outer events showed him a way out.

The inner event, as one might surmise, was a "great" dream. It dealt with Jung's being "caught in the seventeenth century." While he did not recognize at first the concrete meaning of the dream, Jung felt that there was something portentous and paradoxical about it; perhaps his "imprisonment" in an earlier era, by restricting his external freedom, would enable him to break his inner bonds. The outer event that led him out of his impasse came through his friendship with Richard Wilhelm, the eminent German scholar of China, who initiated Jung into the mystical mathematics of the *I Ching* and into the magical science of Chinese alchemy.

Fascinated with the *I Ching*, Jung began experimenting with the ancient Chinese oracle that relies on the agency of a bundle of forty-nine yarrow stalks. The person seeking guidance takes the stalks, presents a question, and without counting divides the bundle into two handfuls. This division generates, through an easily followed mechanical procedure, a number of constellations called hexagrams. The meaning of each of the sixty-four possible hexagrams is indicated in a passage in the *I Ching*, the *Book of Changes.* The texts are often opaque and require an effort of interpretation, as a dream does.

Jung was struck by how pertinent many of the *I Ching*'s responses were to the questions he had asked. The number of "lucky hits" fascinated him all the more since it defied rational explanation. Jung gives as an example the case of a young man, overly attached to his mother, who was trying to decide whether to marry a young woman he knew. She seemed a suitable match, but he feared that her pleasing facade was hiding a smothering motherliness. Jung threw the *I Ching* for him. The response was anything but ambiguous. It stated categorically, "The maiden is powerful. One should not marry such a maiden." Some years later, when Jung was writing an introduction for a new English edition of the *I Ching*, he asked the oracle what it thought of its chance of success in the English-speaking world. The oracle replied that it thought it was going to do fine.

Jung pondered the riddle of how separating a bundle of reed stalks, seemingly at random, into two handfuls could have such far-reaching results. How to account for the nexus between the physical and psychic series of events? The ordinary law of causality—of traceable cause and effect—clearly failed here. To view the pertinence of numerous hexagrams as being due to pure chance was a paltry, inadequate attempt at explanation, was, in fact, no explanation at all. Jung saw the parallels between what was manifested in the *I Ching* and astrology or other arts of divination. He struggled for a long time to come up with a principle of explanation that was not completely at odds with Western ways of thinking. Finally he settled on the rather awkward formula of an acausal "synchronicity." As an explanatory principle it was of dubious value for it said either too much or too little. Either it was a mere *descriptive* shorthand for certain observed "meaningful coincidences," or—to the extent that it claimed explanatory power—it failed through its attempt to remain within the rationalistic framework exploded by the very phenomena it dealt with. It posited the existence of something like an "acausal causality" without clarifying the nature of this paradoxical concept. Thus, while Jung's much-cited formula of synchronicity directs our gaze to a puzzling and possibly important state of affairs, it is philosophically sterile. It leads us no further in our thought and understanding —as shown by the inability of Jung's disciples to do more with the formula than just parrot it. It also misleads in claiming a potential rationality for a matter possibly beyond rational comprehension.

While Richard Wilhelm's translation of the *I Ching*, and his commentary on the ancient texts, enriched Jung's understanding of Chinese culture, Wilhelm performed an even more valuable service for Jung by leading him through an odd detour to the study of alchemy, which was to preoccupy Jung throughout the second half of his life. (The fifteen-year-old daughter of a friend once addressed the old Jung as follows: "Herr

Professor, you are so clever. Could you please tell me the shortest path to my life's goal?" Without a moment's hesitation Jung replied, "The detour!") In 1928 Wilhelm induced Jung to collaborate on the publication of *The Secret of the Golden Flower,* a treatise on Chinese alchemy. Through his work on this Chinese "Book of Life," Jung's eyes were opened to medieval European alchemy. Only then did it occur to him what his great dream about his long imprisonment in the seventeenth century was about. At once he instructed an antiquarian in Munich to let him know if any books on alchemy happened to come his way.

In alchemy Jung found at last the spiritual ground, and the bridge to Gnosticism, he had been seeking for nearly a decade. Alchemy endowed his analytic psychology with the breadth and depth it needed, by providing an intellectual framework that dated from another era. Jung discovered a startling resonance, almost an identity, between alchemic symbols and the imagery emanating from his own and his patients' unconscious. By making contact with this great, rich body of knowledge and myth (even if it was defamed as ludicrous by the twentieth century), Jung found his own way of seeing things affirmed. And alchemy offered the proper distance, in time and in space, culturally and historically: it was rooted in a European tradition that, unlike Gnosticism, was not so remote as to be beyond the possibility of resurrection. There, in the fertile material of alchemy, were nodal points of the same themes Jung would be engrossed with for the rest of his life: the themes of the numen and the God-man, of timeless archaic images and myths of life's meaning, of the journey of life as a quest for selfhood, and of the mystery of "conjunction" as the marriage and the transcendence of spiritual opposites.

Jung found his spiritual guide to the realm of medieval alchemy in the mighty and scurrilous figure of his countryman Philippus Aureolus Theophrastus Bombast von Hohenheim, called Paracelsus. Decried by his enemies as the Medical Luther, and self-proclaimed as the "Monarch of Physic," Paracelsus was a founder of chemotherapy, precursor of homeopathy, magician, mystic, natural philosopher, miracle doctor—and alchemist. This gargantuan Renaissance man, born near the Swiss village of Einsiedeln, was full to overflowing with what Jung viewed as a Swiss national trait: a spirit of fierce independence. But Paracelsus was a first-generation Swiss. His father, Wilhelm Bombast, was German, the illegitimate and impoverished son of a Swabian aristocrat. Jung attributed Bombast's settling in a remote Swiss valley to his illegitimacy, which he saw as determining both the father's and the son's fate. For the son, according to Jung, took over his father's resentment and quarreled throughout his life with all authorities. Paracelsus apparently felt his destiny so inextricably bound up with that of his misused father that, "in keeping with a tragic law," he had to fall out with everyone else. Such self-caused ostracism, Jung held, was the unavoidable punishment for psychic inbreeding. Does Jung reveal here, in interpreting Paracelsus' story, a buried piece of his own psychic history? Perhaps Jung's open disdain toward his father was only the deceptive (and self-deceptive) facade of a deep, anguished devotion.[1]

Jung had much sympathy for the caustic pugnacity of this outrageous doctor-philosopher who ventured through Europe

[1]Some anecdotal evidence points that way. When a friend inquired from the old Jung about the most moving event in his life, the latter replied: "I can tell you right away. Some time ago, I went sailing on a Sunday on the lake. It was about noon; no one around for miles and miles; clear blue sky. I dozed off. Suddenly my father comes up and pats me on the back, saying, 'Thank you, son, you have done well.'"

and Asia as a sort of itinerant miracle worker. He approvingly cited Paracelsus' motto: "He who can be his own, should not be another's"—a "good and true Swiss motto," Jung noted. A prickly sensitivity, more or less controlled in Jung, was magnified to the point of petulance in Paracelsus, who dripped with vitriolic jibes. A favorite target of his taunts were the universities with their dry-as-dust scholasticism. Looking back upon his student days, he wrote that he wondered how "the high colleges managed to produce so many high asses." When he was made a professor at the University of Basel, he scandalized the authorities by inviting not only students but anyone and everyone to attend his lecture. Wherever he stopped, he would soon be at war with the local powers-that-be and have to wander on again, usually destitute, often having to beg, until he came to the next town, where his fame as a healer would have preceded him. But shortly after his arrival that fame would wither in the blasts of his asperity, and the cycle would start again.

Besides being a great medical reformer, who exalted the healing powers of nature and raged against the medical malpractices of his day, Paracelsus was also a philosopher and alchemist of note. In sharp contrast to modern practice, he saw disease not as some hateful foreign body to be rooted out by any means but as "a natural growth, a seed, something spiritual and living." He reads sometimes like a proponent of what nowadays is called "psychosomatic" medicine, except that for him illness had a spiritual status in a religious cosmology. This did not keep him from fighting the narrow astrological determinism of his day, which saw all the parts of the human body controlled by the stars and planets, and from inquiring into the natural causes of diseases. These inquiries led him to state that "miners' disease" (silicosis) resulted from inhaling metal vapors and was not a punishment for sin administered by mountain spirits. But in the overall scheme of things he saw God as the Chief Pharmacist in a universe permeated with healing powers.

As for alchemy, Paracelsus prized it not only for its knowledge of chemistry, mineralogy, and pharmacology (to which he contributed greatly) but also for its magical secret doctrine. His dictum, "Magick is a Great Hidden Wisdom—Reason is a Great Open Folly," reflected the alchemic view that the realms of physics and metaphysics were magically intertwined by virtue of being endowed with transcendental identity. Thus, apparently mundane chemical operations were at the same time "symbolic" gestures, were, in fact, part and parcel of a psychic chemistry. The complex distillations in flasks and retorts through which the secret elixirs were prepared also promoted the spiritual growth of the adept.

In those days everything was still animate or pure nature; stones and metals could sicken just as animals and people do. The esoteric doctrine of alchemy provided not only means to cure physical evils and to purify gross matter, but also a method of illumination. Alchemy boldly embraced the entire cosmos— God, angels, demons, man, plant and animal creatures, inorganic matter—and saw even in the dullest, tiniest fragment of this totality a microcosm mirroring the macrocosm in all its splendor. "Man is a sun and a moon and a heaven filled with stars," Paracelsus wrote, and he held that the creative energy of the human psyche dwelt in its faculty of imagination: "Resolute Imagination can accomplish all things. . . . Medicine uses imagination strongly fixed."

Jung may have partly misread Paracelsus' and others' alchemical texts and may have bent them to his own purposes, but he was inspired by this rough, erudite, widely traveled miracle worker who railed at official medicine and propounded a form of psychotherapy focusing on the powers of Resolute Imagination. Jung saw in Paracelsus the forerunner of Goethe's *Faust* and Nietzsche's superman, one of those standard-bearers and energy transformers who stand like stylites on the thresholds of new realms of knowledge.

Medieval alchemy has often been equated with the attempt to transmute base metals, such as lead, into gold. But alchemy was much more than a pseudo-science of gold-making with its inevitable cortege of charlatanism. Kenneth Rexroth called it "a subject not just mystifying," but "intrinsically improbable" to the twentieth-century mind. "It is as though a textbook of chemistry, another of mining engineering, another of gymnastics and breathing exercises, another of pharmacology, several sex manuals, and many treatises of transcendental mysticism had been torn to pieces and not just mixed up together, but fused into a totally new chemical compound of thought." In addition, alchemical works were also recipe books in the art of fraud. They are hard for the modern reader to decipher not only because of the cultural distance and their often abstruse verbiage, but also because more often than not they were self-consciously esoteric and intentionally misleading, trying to conceal from all but a few initiates what they ostensibly set out to reveal—the doctrine and practice of alchemy. Thus it is not surprising that Jung had to fill innumerable notebooks with excerpts, tentative translations of recurring alchemical symbols, and many-threaded cross references before he could begin to make sense out of the opaque material. But he was undaunted by such difficulties; the relative inaccessibility of alchemy may have been, in fact, one of its major attractions in Jung's eyes.

Many modern writers on alchemy deny that such a thing as spiritual alchemy ever existed. They accuse Jung of falsely spiritualizing what was at bottom a precursor of modern natural science and of denying the reality of the material processes described by the alchemists. But, as was true in the realm of religion, Jung more or less elegantly sidestepped the crucial problem whether the phenomena in question were real by focusing on the psychic processes which register and interpret those phenomena. To make alchemy serve his purposes, Jung had to emphasize its psychic and symbolic aspects. He held that the alchemists *projected* their own unconscious processes and images into the material events they described. Alchemy was to him "a grand projection-canvas," a "wonderful resource" for decoding the symbolic language of the unconscious.

Noting the parallels between the profuse alchemic iconography and the dreams and fantasies of his patients, Jung concluded that both were manifestations of the "collective unconscious." But the alchemist, being psychologically—though not spiritually—more naive than the modern Westerner, projected his archetypal images upon the obscure inorganic matter he was striving to transmute in his flasks and retorts. In other words, the inorganic substances whose properties had not yet been articulated by empirical science functioned for him as if they were some medieval equivalent of Rorschach inkblots. That at least was Jung's—rather debatable—view on the subject. He wrote that what the alchemist sees in his *materia* "are chiefly the data of his own consciousness which he is projecting into it." The alchemists were, according to Jung, entirely unaware of this process of projection. They failed to realize that they themselves had put into physical matter the attributes and potential meanings that they "discovered" in it. This was particularly true, Jung held, of classical alchemy where empirical science and metascience were almost wholly undifferentiated.

According to Jung, this "unconscious" projection paralleled a consciously held system of symbolic references interpreting chemical operations in a spiritualist vein. In this perspective, the profane attempts to make gold signified, "actually," the search for the philosopher's stone, both material and spiritual in nature; the manifest chemical manipulation was at the same time, and more importantly, a self-manipulation, aiming to produce, by means of a mystical inner transmutation, the psychic gold of purified selfhood. The arduous "great work" of the alchemists, we are told, was part of a regime of spiritual exercises.

The reader may recall that in adolescence Carl Jung daydreamed about transforming an ineffable something drawn from the atmosphere into solid gold. When three decades later he began to immerse himself in the apparently abstruse work of the alchemists, he hoped that his imprisonment in the medieval world would further not only his therapeutic understanding, but also his quasi-mystical quest for the image of the God-man within him. In alchemy he did find echoes, and more than echoes, of the undogmatic, tailor-made religiosity based on personal revelation that he needed, and he also found there the symbolic imagery that was equally necessary to him.

In his first lectures and essays on alchemy, Jung set out to demonstrate how a series of dreams of contemporary people on the road to individuation paralleled the various stations of the hermetic path laid out by the alchemists. Jung harked back to the summons of the sixteenth-century alchemist, Gerhard Dohrn: "You shall change yourselves into living philosophers' stones!" Jung mined in particular a lode of spiritual alchemy that was rooted in Christian—and partly in Gnostic Christian —mysticism and that decoded alchemical images in terms of Christian iconography, interpreting, for instance, the philosophers' stone as a symbol of Christ.

According to alchemical sources, alchemy is a body of doctrine that has on more than one occasion come into the possession of man but has always again been lost. Was Carl Jung a genuine rediscoverer of alchemy? Or did he, as a number of modern writers on alchemy claim, misread the alchemical texts, *projecting* his own presuppositions into a submerged and obscure tradition which he mistreated by treating it as a vast projective system? Since he was himself rampant with projectivity, he well may have. But if so, his misreading was fruitful for Carl Jung in that it provided him with the historical sanction he thought he needed and with the kind of infinitely detailed, convoluted, esoteric imagery consonant with his cognitive style.

14

TWO WELL-TEMPERED FRIENDSHIPS

During the late 1920s and the 1930s, when he was immersed in his alchemical studies, Jung was also very active in the public arena. He undertook numerous lecture tours, organized seminars—mostly in English—at the Psychological Club, taught at the E.T.H. (Institute of Technology) in Zurich, received an honorary degree from Harvard at its tercentenary, delivered the Terry lectures at Yale, and traveled as guest of the British government to India, where he chalked up three more honorary degrees. He also got embroiled in political controversy by becoming, under questionable circumstances, president of the Nazified *General Medical Society for Psychotherapy*. Meanwhile the circle of his students, followers, visitors, and acquaintances from all over the world expanded, and so did his

C. G. Jung—The Haunted Prophet

worldwide correspondence, which he conducted in three languages. The intellectual yield of these years was recorded in several volumes' worth of articles, essays, and lectures. Not until 1944, however, did Jung publish any work comparable in range and bulk to *Psychological Types*, which had come almost a quarter of a century earlier. *Psychology and Alchemy* was the first major product of Jung's years of work with alchemy.

This alchemical period of Jung witnessed also two important friendships: his friendship with Richard Wilhelm, the mediator of the Golden Flower's subtle fragrance, and that with Hermann Graf Keyserling, aristocratic philosopher and culture broker, at whose "School of Wisdom" in Darmstadt, Germany, Jung first met Wilhelm. Both men were contemporaries of Jung.

Jung said that his slowly evolving friendship with Wilhelm, "the peerless teacher," released him from his almost unbearable sense of isolation. This new friendship, like that with Freud, was carried on mainly through letters, and, as in Freud's case, the initiatives toward greater closeness seem to have come chiefly from Jung's partner. Jung was grateful for Wilhelm's tokens of friendship, yet one gets the impression that, despite its cordial tone, it was one of those well-tempered friendships Jung favored from then on—mostly with noted scholars who did not work in Jung's own field but could enrich his mind through their knowledge. However important Wilhelm, Keyserling, Zimmer, Pauli, and Kerenyi may have been for Jung as intellectual catalysts, emotionally his engagement with them remained rather shallow.

Jung prized Wilhelm in particular as an intermediary between East and West, as a messenger from China, whose limpid language exhaled the "plantlike naivete" of the Chinese spirit. When the two men first met, Wilhelm had just returned from a long stay in China where he had gone as a Christian missionary, only to find himself converted to Chinese ways of thinking. Jung sensed with some anxiety that his new friend was caught in a deep spiritual crisis. Wilhelm had been trained as a theologian, and after his return to Germany his earlier, apparently forgotten "Weltanschauung" reasserted itself. What was particularly ominous in Jung's eyes was that Wilhelm himself seemed unaware of the extent of this reversion.

In his letters, Jung showed great concern for Wilhelm's delicate physical health. He did not hesitate to dwell on such mundane topics as a "fatal" Spanish mayonnaise that had "spoiled our precautions" (for Wilhelm's well-being). He sighed that the world devoured the spirit's frail bearers from the inside out, if it did not succeed in destroying them from the outside in. If Jung showed himself so anxious, he wrote, it was because Wilhelm was *too important* for the Western world to let himself be ruined in this manner. ". . . let even evil desires pin you to the earth, so that your work can go on," Jung implored, admonishing his friend to avoid overwork and countries like Spain, where they make mayonnaises that "poison souls and bowels."

Jung felt triumphant when he heard in the spring of 1929 that Wilhelm would be invited to address the German Psychotherapy Society at their next convention. Jung viewed it as a historic event that Wilhelm would be able to inject a large dose of Eastern wisdom into the assembled psychiatrists, who might prove less arrogant and more receptive, Jung thought, than theologians or professional philosophers. He was worried lest some evil-minded demons trip up Wilhelm and warned him once more of the danger to his health arising from the spirit's "unpleasant penchant to consume the body."

Unfortunately, Jung's dismal forebodings came to pass. Wilhelm suffered a relapse of the amoebic dysentery he had contracted in China (and that Jung was to come down with ten years later in India). As the disease worsened, Wilhelm had to enter a Frankfurt hospital, where Jung found him on his death bed. In the hospital Wilhelm began having intense dreams about China, which had disappeared from his dream life for a while. The dreams were altogether sad and mournful.

Richard Wilhelm died on March 1, 1930, one month before he was to have lectured at the Psychotherapy convention. Jung was aggrieved at losing so soon the companion whose undemanding friendship he had valued. In a memorial speech Jung paid a moving tribute to his friend. As was his wont, he viewed Wilhelm's fatal illness as convergent with a spiritual crisis, namely, with the reassertion of the European heritage he had once sacrificed. "Therefore a spiritual crisis of such scope often means death if it takes place in a body weakened by disease. For now the sacrificial knife is in the hand of what was sacrificed, and a death is demanded of the erstwhile sacrificer."

The loss of Richard Wilhelm strengthened Jung's ties to Hermann Graf Keyserling, who for a while became important to him as stimulus, goad, and correspondent. Keyserling was a Russian aristocrat of Baltic origin, who had been forced to Germany by the Bolshevik October Revolution. Enamored of philosophy, a restless culture entrepreneur, he was a superintellectual, a man who in Jung's opinion lived too exclusively in his head. He wandered over the entire globe, endeavoring to meet the most prominent men of each country and recording his experiences, observations, encounters, thoughts, and ruminations in an endless stream of essays and books. For him it was an absolute necessity to be always setting things down in words; he had to see his thoughts written out in front of him to discover what they were.

His great notion, and he promoted it with missionary fervor, was to bring about a synthesis of the wealth of Eastern (mostly mystic) and Western thought. It was an undertaking that was in the wind in Europe during the twenties and stirred Jung, too, for a while. To this end, Keyserling founded a "School of Wisdom" in Darmstadt, a sort of latter-day Plato's Academy, where he and others of like or similar mind strove to reach this lofty goal through seminars, lectures, and study groups. The school had a fairly checkered career; it mirrored all the ambiguity, discord, callowness, and rough edges in its founder's breast. Even its name was characteristic of the count who, being rather inclined toward perversity, once explained that his academy was called the "School of Wisdom" because, first, it was not a school, and second, wisdom was not something that could be taught. Nevertheless, for several years this academy provided a forum for leading Western and Eastern intellectuals, among them Carl Jung.

Like many others, Keyserling first became aware of Jung in the early twenties through *Psychological Types*. Even though impatient with Jung's inability to articulate his intuitions clearly, he found the book an "eye opener." It had a liberating effect on him; its vindication of sensitive, intellectually inclined esthetes—types whose standing was not high where the count had come from—validated his personality. From Jung, Keyserling received "scientific" grounds for liking himself better.

Keyserling initiated contact with the author of this interesting work. The two men met and became friends, but—as Keyserling himself noted—even after they had known each other for years, a true intimacy never developed between them. Keyserling would often complain about how difficult it was to get close to Jung, especially if one approached him on a basis of equality rather than as a wide-eyed adept. He thought that perhaps the earth-bound Jung felt out of his element with the "daring generosity of the aristocrat" and the "high-flyer of the mind," whom Keyserling saw himself as. But he also recognized behind Jung's crusty exterior a "soul of supreme sensitivity," which skillfully eluded whatever was not congenial to it and hid behind a thick protective shell. It did not escape Keyserling's notice that Jung usually appeared at the Darmstadt conferences with a sort of bodyguard, mostly women. (When someone called Jung's attention to the preponderance of women among his pupils, Jung laughingly replied that the psyche, the "anima," is also feminine in gender and that psychology therefore is essentially a woman's affair—a bon mot that, like many of Jung's aphorisms, does not wear too well.) Keyserling also saw through Jung's sometimes brutal cynicism as a defense against his extreme vulnerability.

In general, Keyserling's cool, yet not unsympathetic attitude enabled him to make some astute observations about Jung. Decades before Jung's autobiography provided such startling proof, he recognized that Jung was basically what the Germans call a "spinner," or, as Keyserling phrased it, "an owlish fellow." He saw that Jung's dream life mattered more to him than what happened in his waking hours. While others dream at night of the events of the day, Jung was—even awake—passionately involved with the events of his dreams. As Keyserling saw it, life for Jung was quite literally a dream.

Long before Jung published his first work on alchemy, Keyserling also recognized that despite Jung's cramped attempts at camouflage behind a strict scientism, what was essential was his mystic relationship to the transcendental. Keyserling even gave credence to the rumor that for years Jung had been praying in secret to the god Abraxas, a hermaphroditic figure from the

Gnostic era. He saw the intense conflict between Jung, the creature of the earth, bound to it and at the least provocation professing a pagan nature worship, and the other Jung, striving with every fiber of his being toward those "higher reaches," in which he never felt at home, and whose blinding radiance he had to filter through his psychologism.

But Keyserling also conceded that Jung could sometimes see with uncanny depth into the very essence of another personality. Thus he felt himself admirably understood when Jung noted that a striking aspect of his personality was its almost total lack of the "persona," the socially defined role so important in everyday life. In fact, the count was often in trouble because of this shortcoming. When he asked Jung for advice, Jung replied with a prime example of his humor: "I do not understand your difficulty. In one half-hour a woman comes to me—and I'm her mother; an hour later another one comes—and I'm her lover; then a man comes—and I'm his great-grandmother." He played all these roles quite naturally, he felt, and added, "If a delegation came to me tomorrow and offered me the crown of Switzerland, I would seriously consider whether I had the right to refuse the role of king of Switzerland." But, alas, the crown of Switzerland was never proffered.

Jung's occasional outbursts at his intellectuality Keyserling attributed to the envy of a fox who "eyes the flight of a bird from his den." And Jung did frequently warn the count of the danger of hyperintellectuality. In the late twenties when Keyserling published his book *Spectrum Europa*, in which he undertook a frontal attack on sacred prejudices of Europe and America, Jung wrote to say that he, too, had once stormed the heavens and had worshiped Nietzsche's proud "amor fati." But then it had come to be too much for him and he had built himself his little house "far away by the mountain," and with the retreat had, so to speak, "dis-identified" himself from God. Much as he despised the dominion of the everyday world, he was afraid of it. To fight its sway incessantly would break him before his time. Thus he feared for his ambitious friend.

In this same letter Jung also took up the theme which—as in his letters to Richard Wilhelm—ran like a leitmotiv throughout their correspondence: the theme of his friend's health. The count, whose constitution was not the best, and who was quite often ailing, was suffering the aftereffects of some disease at the time. Jung welcomed the illness, he said, because it forced Keyserling to turn back into himself as he wished him to. With this illness, Jung held, Keyserling paid the earth a salutary tribute, and it was to be hoped that the gods would be so mercifully inclined next time.

There seemed, as things went, to be no lack of this dubious beneficence from the gods. A few months later Jung would again advise the "most respected count" that he must take particular care of his health. Namely, his "extroversion, ranging over all the continents," was using up his body's energy and weakening its resistance. Thus, "stomach ulcers, intestinal disturbances, and infections (especially skin diseases) are not rare among intuitive people." The Graf's enthusiasm for these heavy-handed psychological interpretations of his illness was strictly limited. He felt misunderstood in his intellectuality but continued the correspondence, which still seemed of some value.

The next year he happened to go to South America, where he had a misadventure with a woman author. It led to all manner of emotional turmoil, and he turned to Jung for advice. Jung replied that the fatal interlude Keyserling described had apparently involved a very significant "anima-animus adventure." Such encounters must inevitably end in disappointment, for Keyserling—and his inamorata—had confused the projection of the image of their own souls with the "poor little human creature, who unconsciously functioned as symbol bearer." Although this double comedy of errors was a hellish torment for both people, it also contained a salutary lesson—that one must learn to distinguish between one's anima- (or animus-) image and its human counterpart. Thus Jung did not hesitate to say that this particular torment was an experience he had long wished for Keyserling and added that such agonies were the "most fitting torture" for the hot-blooded, demon-infested earth-woman who had made things so difficult for the poor Graf in South America. Jung closed his letter with the admonition: "All too quickly we make personal tragedy out of what, in the final reckoning, is 'Divine Comedy,' and a spark of eternal flame is then doused in a little puddle."

A few letters later the subject of Keyserling's health came up again. The Graf told Jung that he was pursued by the thought of death, as heart and lung ailments had led to a state of exhaustion; Jung persisted in his psychosomatic interpretation. He was convinced that the collision with the exotic world of South America and the fatal woman of the earth had mobilized Keyserling's unconscious; the man who had lived only in his mind found himself now moved by endopsychic powers whose presence he had never before admitted. Such agitation in the unconscious might very well lead to physical illness. It was Keyserling's duty, Jung wrote, to tune out his overbearing consciousness and listen quietly inside. He should focus on the images appearing before his inner eye or the words his vocal cords wanted to form, and record his fantasies in protocols or drawings. By this Jung-tested method he would be able to tame his unconscious.

Keyserling felt increasingly ill at ease with Jung's insistence on the psychic causation of physical illness. This psychologism seemed to deny the autonomy of the mind so important to Keyserling. Nor could the count get very far with Jung's libido concept. To him it was a physicalistic vestige of the nineteenth century that did not belong in psychology. At last he declared that the body-mind nexus posited by Jung did not exist at all. Jung was myopic in this regard, said Keyserling; by proclaiming himself a pure scientist, he documented his inability to take a genuine philosophical stance. Jung's defects as a thinker also hampered, in Keyserling's increasingly critical view, his efforts to decode the universal language of symbols; at the most, Jung had made some shaky overtures in sketching a grammar and syntax of psychic language. But Jung's formulas were unlikely to survive for long, the more so as Jung, with advancing age, seemed increasingly bogged down in conceptual quagmires.

Keyserling also became more openly critical of Jung's practical suggestions. He charged that they had often been extremely destructive. "With his invectives of the year 1934, Jung expressed, with the deadly instinct of a digger-wasp, precisely what was most hurtful to me in that situation (while in other respects he was completely misleading). And he never perceived what he did, so that in the end I had to laughingly forgive him, for surely he did not consciously want to harm me." Some time later, regarding the tragic lot of the German Jungian, Oscar A. H. Schmitz, Keyserling repeated that Jung would on occasion lapse into treating people he probably did not mean to harm in a manner that would "injure them as fatally as the sting of a digger-wasp striking the ganglia of a caterpillar."

As Keyserling's criticism of Jung increased, so did the distance between the two men. For his part, Jung, who could be quite hamfisted in his missives, did not refrain from jibes and invective. He would accuse Keyserling of callousness and tactlessness in letters that were not exactly models of tact and empathy. So it gradually came to the inevitable estrangement. Since their human contact had never been very deep, there was no dramatic rupture. Their correspondence became simply less frequent, shorter, emptier, and finally dried up altogether.

Jung found less critical foils and brokers for his ideas. Among these, a special place soon belonged to an active, enterprising, rather oversolicitous woman who was born in Budapest in 1890 and by the late twenties was heading the Austrian Cultural League. She repeatedly invited Jung to lecture in Vienna and entertained him with "royal hospitality" (Jung's words) in her home. This was Jolan Jacobi, who twenty years later was the moving force behind the founding of the C. G. Jung Institute.

15

THE FLIRT WITH
THE DEVIL

While Jung sat in his study, trying to wrest the secrets of medieval alchemists from the folios of the *Artis Auriferae*, neighboring Germany witnessed the Nazi upheaval which Hermann Rauschning was later to unmask as "the revolution of nihilism." A political romantic, Jung—like so many others who would later deny it—initially welcomed this revolution. The matter of his collusion with a Nazified, Aryanized German psychiatry forms one of the most shady, least glorious chapters in Jung's entire career.

Let us state at the outset that Jung was not, as his more incensed critics have charged, either a fascist or an anti-semite, in the usual sense. It is true that for a time he beheld the phenomenon of Nazism with fascinated benevolence and said

C. G. Jung—The Haunted Prophet

so. His statements enabled his foes to string together quotations that seemed to brand Jung as at least a temporary fellow-traveler of the Nazis. Yet as compromising as Jung's statements —in or out of context—appear, and as much as he later grew to regret ever having made them, it is far too simplistic to classify him as an outright Nazi.

Jung viewed himself as basically "apolitical" in that he gave politics a role secondary to what he deemed the chief business of human beings (those who really counted, anyway): the personal path toward selfhood. True, he never denied the kingdom of Caesar, and its power to enforce its rules, by terror if need be, but his real concern was with "the kingdom within."

He liked to imagine himself the inveterate Swiss, with all the attendant faults and virtues, among the latter being a deep respect for the democratic institutions of his native land. Yet the tone of this self-declared democrat was often suspiciously aristocratic.[1] Not only did he repeatedly ascribe aristocratic principles to "nature," but he regularly expressed in his letters and verbal utterances profound contempt for the "masses" and the "man-in-the-crowd." Evidently, more was involved here than an assault on the depersonalizing effects of the Industrial Revolution. Despite his veneer of affability, Jung seems to have had little sympathy with the prosaic petit bourgeois or working man. When he told a group of American journalists that he considered oligarchy the best form of government, it was no careless remark. One thing he did share with the Swiss petit bourgeois, though, was a fanatical hatred of Communism, which—as we have already noted—was the constant in his vacillating political opinions. To him, Bolshevism was the devil

[1]Such contradictions meant little to a man in whose mind paradox had been elevated to the status of a supreme principle.

incarnate because it appeared to push the leveling of individuality to its furthest extreme, because of its totalitarian usurpation of the religious sphere, because of its technocratic rationalism, and, not least of all, because of its godless irreverence for the sacred property rights of persons like himself. And so, toward the close of the thirties, when the specter of Hitler had finally become unsettling, Jung dreamed the dream of every Western anti-Bolshevist of the time, of enlisting Hitler's dynamism in a crusade against the Soviet Union.

But anti-Bolshevism is not in itself fascism. If we are ever to understand Jung's flirtation with Nazism (and fascism), we must look around for other, deeper motives. Jung's romanticism was one. Initially, he saw the National-Socialistic "movement" as a powerful eruption of the very collective unconscious he had postulated. Murmurings in the primeval forest of the Germanic soul had swollen into a gale of world-shaking force; the demons who seemed to have been secured in the dungeons of collective oblivion had risen up again, just as Jung had long predicted they would. He was confirmed in his role as seer and in his profound contempt for the unholy rationalism that had triumphed in the world for so long. For no matter how ideologically confused Hitlerism might appear, no one could accuse it of siding with rationalism.

There were, in the Nazis' "blood and soil" mysticism, all manner of things that would sooner attract than scare off a romantic like Jung. The reawakening of the "blond beast," heralded by Jung's favorite philosopher Nietzsche, that frail figure who dreamed of the Superman, filled Jung with a reverence not free of horror. With barely masked sympathy, he wrote in 1934 of the "formidable phenomenon of National Socialism," which the world (meaning Jung) beheld "wide-eyed with astonishment," and asked rhetorically whether this historic happening might not undeceive the misguided followers of Freud's semitic psychology. He openly admired the reversion of German youth to unadorned paganism, complete with ritual sacrifices of sheep at solstice. He talked about their predecessors, the *Wandervögel* of the Weimar Republic, those blond youths with lute and knapsack "who were to be seen as restless wanderers on every road from the North Cape to Sicily. . . ." He described how, toward the close of the Weimar period, the place of the wanderer had been usurped by the armies of the unemployed that lined every country road in Germany, and how Hitler had transformed this aimless wandering into the highly organized (though equally aimless) marching of hundreds of thousands of men, how he had "literally set all Germany on its feet." Jung saw this restlessness as evidence of the rebirth of the old Germanic god Wotan, who had disappeared when his oaks had fallen and who now celebrated his resurrection in an age when "the Christian God had proved too weak to save Christendom from fratricidal slaughter." While the Holy Father in Rome impotently bemoaned the fate of his divided flock to his God, the ancient, one-eyed hunter stood laughing at the edge of the German forest, throwing the saddle over Sleipnir, his eight-legged gray steed. God of storm and frenzy, ceaseless wanderer, hunter, unleasher of passion and lust for war, conjurer and master of illusion, Wotan was what Jung saw moving in the "formidable phenomenon" of National Socialism. "As an autonomous archetype Wotan produces effects in the collective life of a people and thereby reveals his own nature." The astounding transformation of Germany had been made by this god of the wind, which "bestoweth where it listeth, and thou hearest the sound thereof, but canst not tell whence it cometh nor whither it goeth." This wind-god "seizes everything in its path and overthrows all that is not firmly rooted. When the wind blows it shakes everything without or within."

Hand-in-hand with his belief in the reawakening of Wotan from his thousand-year sleep went Jung's preoccupation with the myth of the hero, which had already been given a central role in his earlier work. In an essay written in 1932 and printed two years later, he celebrated the "leader personality" as the source of all grand, liberating events of history and contrasted to it the "ever secondary, lazy masses, who cannot make the least move in the absence of a demagogue." The jubilation of Italy was for the personality of Mussolini, while the lamentations of others were for their lack of great leaders. And in a revealing, hardly ambiguous footnote, added to the 1934 printing of the essay, Jung wrote: "Since this sentence was first written, Germany, too, has found its leader" (Führer).

When in 1933 fate beckoned, as it were, Jung did not resist the call and himself became a minor leader, an officially sanctioned Führer of the mind. Shortly after the Nazi seizure of power, Ernst Kretschmer resigned as president of the German *General Society for Psychotherapy*, only to be succeeded by the Swiss democrat. Criticized later for his action, Jung offered the excuse—the age-old cant of the hanger-on—that he had simply bowed to the wishes of his German colleagues, who hoped to save the delicate seedling of psychotherapy from being trampled underfoot by the Nazi state. But we need only remember the Jung who fantasized to Keyserling of being offered the crown of Switzerland by his fellow citizens; the Jung who felt, not without resentment, that he had been neglected, isolated, and misunderstood; the Jung whose theories reaped little attention at home and, abroad, only a small fraction of that garnered by Freudian psychoanalysis; the Jung who was subject to frequent outbursts of gall and rage and who was not wholly immune to the enticements of power: against this background, his willingness to head an organization that had been Nazified, and whose members were presumed to be thoroughly familiar with Hitler's *Mein Kampf*, appears in a very dubious light.

What, we may ask, was the content of Jung's first editorial for the *Zentralblatt*, the journal of the group he was now heading? He wrote: "In the interest of science, we can no longer ignore the palpable differences, long known to persons of insight, between the Germanic [note: not simply 'German'] and Jewish psychologies. Psychology, more than any other science, contains a personal factor, ignorance of which falsifies the results of theory and practice."

Jung later defended these remarks on the grounds that he had merely been repeating what he had always written and espoused. But was this really the proper moment for lending support to the racist mania of brown-shirted despots who would soon organize pogroms and worse? Was this the time for Jung to confer on these bullies whatever measure of scientific prestige he enjoyed? It hardly seems plausible that Jung, often so sensitive to political stirrings, was in this instance totally unsuspecting of a political situation that precluded discussion of his hypotheses and gave them the character of a threat, if not a provocation. This was, in any case, the view held by many of his colleagues. They found a spokesman in the Zurich psychoanalyst Gustav Bally, who asked in the *Neue Zürcher Zeitung* what Jung had aimed to accomplish with his editorial. To what actions was he trying to incite his colleagues? And wherein lay the fateful distinction between Jewish psychotherapy and the Germanic variety Jung foresaw as the savior of the discipline? To these and similar questions, Bally wrote, Jung had not given an explicit reply. But "Jung does not need to reply; his reply is inherent in the situation itself. Anyone who chooses to bring up the racial issue from a position as editor of a nazified journal must realize that his challenge is issued against a backdrop of organized emotions that will give it—nay, has already given it—the meaning implicit in its formulation." In fact, Walter Cimbal, German coeditor of the *Zentralblatt*, had already confirmed this view by referring directly to Jung's statement in announcing that work had begun toward instituting a purely German psychology and psychotherapy.

Did Jung really champion a Germanic, "Jew-free" psychotherapy before the time when German cafés and other public places were cleansed of the "intolerable" presence of Jews? As unnerving and, ultimately, misleading as this picture is, Jung's behavior nevertheless gives it a certain air of plausibility. In a 1934 issue of the *Zentralblatt*, he published a programmatic denunciation of Sigmund Freud's "subversive" semitic psychoanalysis. The reader need not be equipped with radar to pick up the National-Socialistic overtones of the article. The reigning politics having evidently put wind in the sails of Jung's polemic against his former mentor, Jung sets the "Aryan" unconscious up against its Jewish counterpart.[2] To the former he attributes "the potential energy and creative seeds of a future still awaiting fulfillment," an assessment which, he warns, "it is dangerous to dismiss as mere nursery-school romanticism." Alongside the future-laden collective unconscious of the "still youthful Germanic peoples," the Jewish

[2]The "collective unconscious," formerly a universal concept, has now been obsequiously altered to the more fashionable lines of a "racial unconscious."

unconscious looks decrepit indeed. It is entirely lacking in creative tension, since the average Jew "is far too conscious and differentiated to go about pregnant with the tensions of unborn futures." Besides, Jewish psychiatry—on which Jung has just performed a hysterectomy—is incapable of plumbing the depths of the Germanic soul. Psychotherapy has been sadly mistaken in "blindly applying Jewish categories . . . to Christian Germans and Slavs." Jewish-inspired psychology has debased the priceless treasure of the Germanic peoples, leaving only a morass of banal infantilisms. Again and again, Jung ominously refers to Freudian psychology as "subversive," "depreciatory," and "undermining." He harps, as if spellbound, on its "obscenity" and "smutty-mindedness." He calls it a "dirty-joke psychology," whose final word, "this is nothing but," reduces complex spiritual states to sexual indecencies and perversions. This is the very method used by the peddler out after a cheap bargain, Jung points out, except that in this case the item up for sale is the soul of a human being, "his hope, his boldest flight, his finest adventure." There is no great distance here between Jung's phraseology and the Nazis' stock-in-trade descriptions of Jews as "alien," "subversive," "lascivious," "parasitic" enemies of the people, creatures bent only on haggling and usury.

In 1934 Jung tried to justify his accommodation with the Nazis by arguing that it was senseless, indeed absurd, to fight an avalanche. His broad gaze, surveying the ages, recognized in the Nazi regime the first rumblings of the "Twilight of the Gods," an apocalyptic destiny—and Jung never was one to oppose whatever he had once defined as destiny. He cautiously remarked, accordingly, that science had no interest in provoking cataclysms but would do better in adjusting to altered circumstances to preserve as much of its heritage as possible.

But was it really only a case of a necessary adaptation to adverse circumstances if in 1938, fully five years after Hitler's seizure of power, Jung could still describe the "Führer" as a man with the look of a visionary, a historical phenomenon belonging to the type of the truly inspired shaman, the loud-speaker of the German soul, a man whose power was "magical" rather than "political," and—lo and behold—a "spiritual vessel"?

When accused on the basis of such utterances of pro-Nazism and anti-semitism, Jung reacted with hurt or rage. Feeling monumentally misunderstood, he stated that any Jew reproaching him with anti-semitism was suffering from paranoia; not everyone who pointed out differences between Jews and non-Jews, or criticized a particular Jew, was for that reason a Jew-hater. To Jewish correspondents who took offense at his remarks, he protested that he had nothing at all against the Jews as a whole. He had attacked Freud not for his Jewishness, but for his materialism, intellectualism, and atheism. In a letter to his Jewish colleague James Kirsch, dated May 1934, he complained of the "stupid gossip" that had made him out to be an anti-semite. Earlier on, he says, he had earned the same accusation from Freud, merely because he could not bring himself to sanction Freud's brand of soulless materialism. There was no one as sensitive to criticism as a Jew—except a German, who likewise equates criticism of one of his kind with criticism of all. In the majority of cases, he, Jung, had gotten along very well with his Jewish patients and colleagues. And Kirsch really should know better than to believe him "capable of the personal folly of anti-semitism." Didn't Kirsch realize the extent to which he saw human beings as individuals, and how he strove to lift them out of their collective bonds? Jung added that he had included an essay by a Jewish writer in his recently published (1934) book *Reality of the Soul* in order to annoy not only the Nazis, but also every Jew who had ever pilloried him as an anti-semite.

It is probably true that Jung's outlook was far too catholic for him to embrace wholeheartedly a narrow racism that was, if nothing else, at odds with his aspirations to universality. Among his most devoted pupils, too many were Jews: Erich Neumann, Gerhard Adler, James Kirsch, Aniela Jaffé, to name only a few. None apparently had been made to feel slighted, or less than equal, on account of his or her Jewishness. And the fact that most of Jung's Jewish pupils remained loyal to him right up to his death, and then beyond it, can hardly be written off as simply another instance of proverbial Jewish self-hatred.

We shall never succeed in accounting for Jung's curious statements during the early Nazi years unless we carefully avoid hurried conclusions. If his initial verdict on Hitler and Nazism was overly lenient, the fault lay, as we have said, in a romanticism that rendered him susceptible to the blandishments of the "hero cult." Later he was to describe this as a grievous error in judgment. By 1939, in any case, he said in a letter to an American correspondent that, from all he had heard, Hitler must be "more than half crazy." Jung's enemies were therefore mistaken in their accusation that he waited for the end of the war to strip Hitler of the divine nimbus. His anti-semitic sounding statements can in turn be attributed largely to the floods of resentment that periodically inundated him—the labile and constricted neurotic—and then overshot their intended target. In the present context this target was undoubtedly Freud, the spiritual father he loved and hated. When his smoldering animosity against Freud erupted, from the very depths of his personality, it swept like lava over anything in its path. Blinded by the intensity of his personal passion, Jung may have failed to realize fully to what extent his denunciations of "Jewish" psychoanalysis played into the hands of men whose goals were far more ambitious—and bloodier—than the defeat of Freudian psychology's claims to validity.

In the previously cited letter to James Kirsch, Jung predicted that his critics, once they had given up trying to pin on him the labels of fascist and anti-semite, would go on to accuse him of "lacking all conviction." This preventive effort reveals a chink in Jung's armor. For in matters of politics—and not only in these—he tended to be highly malleable, if not opportunistic. We need only recall how he suggested to Freud that psychoanalysis might be made palatable to a much wider public if its offensive features were played down, and how this too diplomatic finesse displeased the master. Did a lack of inner firmness make Jung vulnerable to ideological maladies to which sturdier personalities were immune? Do we have here another instance of the two souls in one breast? Apparently so. And if so, one begins to understand how Jung could make an ostensibly anti-semitic statement, and then, in the very next breath, become incensed at the "inane" charge of anti-semitism. It may be not quite accurate to say that Jung was anti-semitic in the company of anti-semites, and pro-semitic in the presence of anti-anti-semites—yet there was something in his make-up that tended in this direction.

16

YEARS OF MISERY

In early 1938 Jung proposed to a number of Zurich analysts that they organize a biweekly colloquium to exchange ideas about depth psychology. Apparently Jung hoped to gain some sympathy for his ideas among the psychiatric guild, whose members had not shown much interest in his work up to then. He made a point of inviting a leading Freudian, Gustav Bally, who had earlier criticized him sharply for his collaboration with Nazis. Another member of the group was Medard Boss, who later made a name for himself as the founder of the school of *Daseinsanalysis.*

As far as Jung could see, all went well at first. He chaired these discussions of clinical cases and dream series, which he thought freewheeling and fruitful. The others appeared to be

C. G. Jung—The Haunted Prophet

intrigued by his thoughts and nodded agreement. What Jung failed to notice was that he dominated these sessions pretty one-sidedly and gave his colleagues little opportunity to challenge his ideas. He did not realize how cutting the tone of his remarks could be and how much his edgy dogmatism grated on the nerves of men who had claims to some thoughts of their own. Particularly grating was his habit of presenting his most speculative hypotheses—like that of the collective unconscious —as unimpeachable empirical facts.

Gradually the atmosphere at Jung's colloquium came to resemble that of the classroom of an overbearing teacher who reduces his students to reciting their lessons. If one of the "students" did speak up, the rest of the "class" was taken aback by such boldness. This happened when Medard Boss dared to ask Jung whether a rather obscure remark of his meant that a therapist should under no circumstances go to bed with a patient. Curtly Jung replied, yes, that was precisely what he meant, and quickly passed on to another topic.

In spite of Boss's outspokenness, Jung was quite fond of him and hence was the more incensed when in the mid-forties Boss published a book that advanced decidedly un-Jungian notions.[1] In this work Boss advocated the use of a phenomenological method in clinical psychiatry, and in its light criticized some of Jung's pet theories. Jung reacted by sending Boss a cross letter. He remarked that Boss's excellent clinical observations "contrasted strikingly" with the level of his theoretical remarks. Once more striking up his old song about being misunderstood by everybody, Jung wrote: "That you deem it necessary to reproach me with a narrow-minded adherence to

[1] *The Meaning and Content of Sexual Perversions*, Hans Huber, Berne, 1947.

causalism is going a bit far. Apparently you do not know that, thirty years ago, I questioned the notion of causality vis-à-vis Freud, with the result that Freud's followers branded me as being beyond the pale of science."

Jung took it very much amiss, he wrote, that Boss had not seen fit to raise his objections in the colloquium. There, he felt, Boss had had ample opportunity to explain his new existentialist method and to demonstrate its superiority. He, Jung, did not want to be put in a position where he appeared to be forcing his "doctrine" (which, he said, wasn't one) down the throats of unwilling colleagues who held discussions behind his back and then documented their lack of understanding in books and public lectures. Such incidents made him wonder whether there was much point in continuing the colloquium.

The tone of Jung's letter was that of a parent hurt by his child's lack of trust. In his reply, Boss tried to reassure Jung that he had not meant to be polemical. Jung was somewhat mollified, but stuck to the pose of the aggrieved parent. He had been "greatly disappointed," he wrote in his next letter, to hear Boss's divergent ideas only indirectly; after all, in the colloquium he had welcomed every one of Boss's suggestions with open arms. He was understandably loath, he explained, to be "maneuvered into a false position" in which he would appear intolerant of dissenters or despotically dogmatic. As to Boss's new-fangled ideas, he quite readily confessed that he did not understand them but declared himself anxious to be enlightened. "One is always glad," he wrote with mock humility, "to hear something new and comprehensive about topics over which one has racked one's brains a long time. I have always marveled at how philosophers manage to say so much that appears to be illuminating about matters they are not familiar with, and why we are too stupid to do likewise. Where does Heidegger get all his knowledge about *the* universal scheme ... I am still quite far from attaining such heights." Once more Jung queried whether it made sense to keep a colloquium going whose members did not speak their mind. In fact, the group disbanded shortly thereafter.

Jung's sally against what he regarded as cheap, frothy, unfounded metaphysics was not without precedent. Heidegger had been for some time a *bête noire* of Jung and gradually became the target of reckless attacks. At first, Jung merely accused him of performing verbal sleight-of-hand. Somewhat later he spoke disparagingly of somebody's "mastery of convoluted banalities," the "Platonic idea" of which he, Jung, found embodied in Heidegger. Next, Heidegger stood accused of hiding his unconscious bias—and his pathology—behind his bombast. A first-year student in psychiatry, Jung said, could easily identify the true lineage of Heidegger's phraseology. His intellectual kin were to be found in mental asylums, as patients and as philosophically incontinent psychiatrists.

Jung found respite from misguided colleagues and airborne metaphysicians in the circle of his devotees. With them he felt safe from criticism, concealed or otherwise, for they did not traffic in such contraband. This circle had been joined in late 1939 by a new convert, a member of one of the richest, most socially prominent American families: Mary Conover Mellon.[2]

---

[2]Jung seemed to exert a strange fascination on American millionaires. Besides the McCormick-Rockefellers and the Mellons, he counted a number of other millionaires among his clientele. To these, he could be quite harsh when he felt that they needed a lesson in humility. He once ordered an American heiress to leave her Rolls-Royce in the Hotel Baur-au-Lac in Zurich and take the train like ordinary mortals when she came to see him. Another one he made sit on the floor during consultation, instead of offering her a chair.

Mary Mellon was the daughter of a well-to-do Kansas physician and a Vassar graduate. Her first marriage, to a magazine writer, ended in divorce. Her second husband, Paul Mellon, head of the Mellon dynasty, presided over a fortune estimated at several hundred million dollars during the 1940s. She sought out Jung because of her lifelong asthma. Reading his books had led her to think that her illness might be psychosomatic. She induced her husband to accompany her on the pilgrimage to the medical magician of Lake Zurich. And like Harold McCormick before him, Paul Mellon soon found himself drawn into the magic circle of Jungian psychology. During the fall and winter of 1939/40 both Mellons attended Jung's seminars, studied his writings, and had long talks with him. They were much taken with Jung's personality and regretted that the turmoil of World War II disrupted their stay and made them return to the States, in the spring of 1940, before they felt ready to leave. They decided to set up a foundation that would publish Jung's work in English, and Mary Mellon worked out the charter of what was to become the Bollingen Foundation.[3]

During the war years, Jung and Mary Mellon stayed in touch through letters which shed light on Jung's state of mind at that time. In June 1940 he wrote a brief, panicky letter, under the impress of a rumor that mail service to the United States would be cut off, now that Hitler had conquered France. He was depressed about the situation created by the German victory: "Night has descended over Europe. Heaven only knows how and when we shall meet again." Early in 1941 Jung wrote Mary that the "damnable war against England and the destruction of France" made him feel miserable. In his own

[3]She thus brought to fruition a project that Edith Rockefeller had conceived, and then allowed to lapse, some twenty years earlier.

country, everything was "as if frozen." People were still moving about and trains running as usual, but underneath this surface of normality there was an undercurrent of fear of a German attack. Such an attack would be sheer madness, "but the Germans are mad." In case of German occupation, he expected to be silenced, which he would not mind, as long as he was left his books and a roof over his head.

Jung's next letter to her, even gloomier in tone, was headed: "Bollingen, 18 April 1941, Anno miseriae." A year of misery, indeed. He felt exhausted and "deeply depressed by the senselessness of this war." Europe was living under a thick black cloud, and there seemed to be no escape from "the soundless pressure of evil and dull idiocy." He took time out from his lamentations, though, to thank Mary Mellon for her labors on behalf of their "common cause." "Little Bollingen at Yale," he wrote. "It is marvelously grotesque."[4] Next he turned to some dreams Mary had reported in a letter. He interpreted them, and then, sounding rather sycophantic, wrote that he was grateful to fate that she had such dreams, "otherwise the world would be rather empty in the Western Hemisphere."

In a letter of that fall to Mary Mellon, Jung's tone became lyrical. He told her how often he thought of her, how often he wished he might see her again. But she was "further away than the moon." Her letters, he said, exuded "an immediate warmth and something like a living substance which has an almost compelling effect." If she were not on the other side of the ocean, he might be tempted to do something foolish. He begged her not to misunderstand him: he was "in a healthy condition of mind," and merely describing the almost uncanny effect her letters had on him, proving that there was a living

---

[4]It was planned at the time to publish the Bollingen Series under the imprint of the Yale University Press.

connection between them, "an unconscious identity," transcending space. His attitude toward her was one "of honest and sincere devotion beyond all doubt." But their psychic connectedness could not undo the stubborn fact that they would be "separated for a long time, perhaps forever, if such a human concept can be applied to whatever happens after death."

Jung's premonition that he might not see Mary Mellon again was borne out by events. Shortly after the end of the war she died, while hunting, in the aftermath of one of those asthma attacks that had made her seek out Jung. She was forty-two years old. At the time of her death, her plans for disseminating Jung's work in America had crystallized, and the Bollingen Foundation had been set up on a firm footing in New York. It was to prove most successful in carrying out its task.

As for Jung, the final years of the war exacted a heavy toll in misery from him. The fact that Switzerland was entirely fenced in by the armies of Hitler and Mussolini and that travel abroad was impossible made him feel claustrophobic. Whatever sympathies he may have had earlier for the Nazi mythology had long gone up in smoke. He was entirely on the side of the Allies, realizing that Hitler's victory would signify the end of everything he held dear. His distress was the more acute as the suspicion of pro-Nazi sentiment continued to hang over him; he could not shake off the specter of his past flirtation.

In the face of the apocalyptic events around him, he had even engaged for a moment in active politics. In the fall of 1939, he had himself listed as a candidate for the Swiss parliament, on the ticket of a party calling itself the Union of Independents.[5] This was a politically amorphous group claim-

[5] *Landesring der Unabhängigen.*

ing to represent the interests of consumers and of the "little guy" in general. Jung had detected popular demand for tribunes who stood for "intellectual values." But this demand must have been less than he thought, for he failed to be elected. He advocated a plan to mobilize all Swiss men between the ages of eighteen and sixty, regardless of whether they were fit for military service. In this way, and by paying civilians no more than soldiers, the social tensions between the men in uniform and those they were charged to defend would be minimized. Some features of Jung's plan eventually found their way into a set of ordinances that partly compensated inductees for loss of income.

Jung called 1940, the year in which France was crushed by Hitler's armies, "the fateful year I have awaited for more than a quarter of a century." He related a prophetic dream that had oppressed him from the time of its occurrence, just before the close of World War I, until the outbreak of the Second World War. In this dream he watched as fire rained down from heaven to consume the cities of Germany. He himself, though covered with burns, managed to escape. Connected to this dream was the dark intimation that 1940 would be the fatal year. Searching for a parallel in world history, Jung ended by comparing 1940 to the cataclysmic year of 26 B.C., when the great temple at Karnak was destroyed by an earthquake; this had proved the prelude to the destruction of all temples. Like the chaotic events of 1940, it had signaled the dawn of a new era. Always fond of astrological schemes, Jung pointed out that 1940 was the year in which the earth was approaching the meridian of the first star of Aquarius. Thus astrology confirmed his foreboding that the battles then raging were the "premonitory rumblings" of an apocalyptic period of transition.

His ears cocked for these rumblings, distraught and, despite his prophetic pronouncements, disoriented, Jung found his capacity for work slackening. For the first time, he began to complain about signs of getting old. His heart felt tired and his liver manifested a growing distaste for major digestive exertions. But with his usual self-discipline, he managed to keep up with his many obligations. His analytic practice still made large claims on him, though now, because of the war, few foreigners made their way to his consulting room. His literary output declined, consisting for a while only of essays. In 1944 he completed a larger work, *Psychology and Alchemy*, but this was more an elaboration of papers previously published than a new departure. That same year, 1944, also gave him a sharp reminder of his mortality, in that he suffered a near-fatal heart attack. But, as we have already seen, Jung read this episode as a warrant of his being immortal.

A ray of light during those gloomy war years was the arrival in Switzerland of Karl Kerényi, a Hungarian philologist. Kerényi, some twenty years Jung's junior, had made a name for himself as an interpreter of Greek mythology. In 1940 he had sent Jung a paper about Persephone, the radiant maiden of Greek legend whose light step upon the dry, brown hillside was enough to make it fresh and verdant. Jung was delighted with the essay and offered to write a psychological commentary. The joint work was published the following year under the title *The Divine Maiden*.

Since Hungary was an ally of Germany, Kerényi was able to travel to Switzerland, where he lectured on Greek mythology before a circle of fascinated listeners. One participant, the essayist Max Rychner, reported to a friend: "There's a nice Hungarian here who knows a lot of exquisite things about the ancient sacraments. Old Carl Jung sits there, puffing his stogy, pencil in hand, and does not let a single word about the mysterious queen of Hades escape him." Rychner compared Kerényi to Ulysses, craftily "hovering over chasms and abysses, at home abroad, never at a loss for his way," versed in the rites of the netherworld.

During the height of the war, this latter-day Ulysses contrived to talk the pro-fascist Hungarian ruler Kallay into sending him to Switzerland on an official mission without time limit. Kallay wanted to take out some belated insurance against the lengthening odds on a German defeat. As an eminent scholar, Professor Kerényi was named Cultural Attaché at the Hungarian Legation in Bernc, the only capital in central Europe that still housed British and American diplomats. The hope was that Kerényi, by showing the flag of Hungarian culture, would soften the attitudes of the soon-to-be victorious Western allies toward his country. It is unlikely, though, that the American Legation in Berne, from where Allen Dulles was then spreading his net of O.S.S. agents over Europe, could have mustered at the time more than a peripheral interest in the achievements of Hungarian culture.

Whether the Americans took note of Kerényi's arrival or not, Jung, at any rate, was pleased that the war had exiled this sprightly decoder of mythologies to Switzerland. He could not find praise enough for Kerényi's ingenious ways of illuminating the darkest corners of Greek and Roman legends. The Hungarian's work, he said, had opened his eyes for the striking parallels between those ancient myths and the imagery of alchemy. It also seemed to confirm, at least in Jung's eyes, his controversial doctrine of the collective unconscious. He found Kerényi's writings a genuine treasure trove, revealing the indescribable riches of Greek mythology—riches previously concealed from him by the pedantry of musty philologists. "You have only to touch the fragments with the magic wand of your intuition," he wrote the Hungarian, "and they readily fall into recognizable forms." The contemplation of the motifs revealed by Kerényi's magic had "intensified and heightened" his life.

Kerényi, for his part, thought highly of Jung's work, without being carried away by his admiration. With his eagle's-eye view, he sought to weave Jung into the fabric of intellectual history. Jung's great contribution, as Kerényi saw it, was to highlight the relevance of depth psychology to modern literature and art. By stressing the playful and dramatic aspects of dreams, their tendency to not only rehearse the past but also to try out the future, Jung had expanded Freud's theory of dreams. Jung had also enlarged the self-understanding of modern man and released him from his monadic isolation by showing the convergence of his dreams with age-old myths.

Kerényi's generous praise of Jung's achievement did not prevent him from pointing out that the poetic spirit of a Thomas Mann, a Rilke, a Hofmannsthal, a D. H. Lawrence, showed visionary powers at least equaling those of Carl Jung. And even Heidegger, whom Jung wanted to relegate to the madhouse, was paid tribute by Kerényi as one of the great initiators of Western man's latest, radical alteration of consciousness.

Jung, who could be very ticklish in matters of prestige, may have felt his halo dimmed by Kerényi's genuflections before rival figures. He had always had a hard time listening to homages to others that might imply a diminution of his own nimbus. Also he cannot have been very pleased at finding himself lumped with Heidegger. At any rate, his feelings for Kerényi gradually cooled, and he found himself once more intellectually orphaned. To be sure, there was always the growing phalanx of his devotees, but their intellectual stature left something to be desired, and their blind, and often quite intrusive, worship got tiresome in the end even for Jung. He really craved the company of people whom he considered his intellectual equals, and on occasion went to some length to make their acquaintance.

One person whom Jung approached was his Geneva compatriot Carl J. Burckhardt, historian, diplomat, and writer of note. In a letter to Burckhardt, Jung proposed a meeting and instructed him to tell no one about it. Burckhardt was mystified by Jung's secretiveness but wrote back that he was willing to see him on his next visit to Zurich. Jung met him at the railway station, a "highly sardonic smile" on his face.[6] Then, at Jung's suggestion, they strolled down the Bahnhofstrasse toward the lake. They sat down on a bench by the water, and before long the two men, who until now had known each other only through their writings, were immersed in lively talk. Already at the station they had begun to grumble in unison how confined they felt in wartime Switzerland. Quickly warming up to the topic, Jung had blurted out: "Sometimes I dream that I am trampling down a Swiss village." He made this confession in the unadulterated Basel dialect he reserved for his countrymen. Despite his conspiratorial staging, Jung apparently had nothing more in mind than to exchange ideas, in dialect, with a man of undeniable stature. Except for Jung's opening confession, the talk did not touch on anything very personal. Yet, like many of Jung's conversations, it ranged widely, touching upon

[6]Burckhardt subsequently described the rendezvous in a letter to a friend.

astrology, religion, metaphysics, and psychology. In between, Jung complained that his work on psychology of religion was detested and misunderstood by Protestants and positivists alike. Having poured out his wrath about the "wretched indolence" of contemporary attitudes, he finally came round to politics. He made some caustic comments about Hitler, whose rule of terror had been prophesied with amazing accuracy by the sixteenth-century astrologer Nostradamus, and about Franklin D. Roosevelt, whom he kept calling "the limping messenger of the apocalypse." He also related to the amazed Burckhardt how the SS-general Heydrich, Hitler's proconsul in occupied Prague, had in a drunken stupor taken a shot at his own mirror image, shouting "At last I have got you, you bastard!" Circling back to psychology, Jung explained that the dreadful inner split bared by this episode was also manifest in the total asymmetry of Heydrich's face.[7]

According to Burckhardt, they might have continued talking for quite a while had the evening not turned chilly, and had a neighboring bench not been occupied, quite by chance, by a "deeply introverted female" whose dissertation-in-progress involved Jung. Although she was obviously less of an archetype than a prototype (namely, of neurotic awkwardness), Jung felt obliged to address a few words to her, and with this interruption Burckhardt's meeting with the Goethe of Lake Zurich came to an end.

The afternoon with Burckhardt was for Jung a rare bright spot in a succession of bleak months and years. "The soundless pressure of evil and dull idiocy" he had registered in one of his letters was wearing him down. While the great conflagration

[7]In a conversation with a visitor during the early forties, Jung twice unwittingly referred to Heydrich as "Heidegger."

of the war impinged but little on his external life, it mightily stirred his apocalyptic imagination, as World War I had done thirty years earlier. The accumulating misery of those war years was soon to climax in the heart attack that brought Jung to the threshold of death and from which he was never completely to recover.

17

THE INSTITUTE—CARL JUNG'S MYSTICAL BODY

The coronary embolism he suffered in 1944 left Jung in a state of physical disarray. "It was then that life busted me," he wrote later, "as sooner or later it busts all of us." He had crossed the threshold into old age. His once erect figure, now thin and brittle, began to droop, had to be braced by a cane. He now truly became the embodiment of the "limping messenger from Lake Zurich" as he liked to mythologize himself. Bouts with illness—new embolisms, intestinal fevers, and liver ailments—became more frequent, requiring each time a longer convalescence, while the periods of his voluntary seclusion in Bollingen also lengthened. Foremost in Jung's mind now were the great riddles of sickness, death, and the meaning of human existence.

He freely admitted to fear of protracted suffering and

wasted little sympathy on those—whether psychiatrists or ministers—who strove to rid people of all anxiety in the belief that it was rooted in some neurosis or other. Such endeavors struck him as foolish, as driven by wishful thinking. For Jung, the primal anguish and trembling that precedes all specific fears was God-given and had to be borne to the bitter end, not blandly evaded. He often felt as if he were doing things for the last time, as if the moment of his death were nearer than it actually turned out to be. In 1947, for the first time in his many years there, he did not feel up to planting corn and potatoes in his patch of black soil in Bollingen. The sight of weeds luxuriating in the orphaned garden made him melancholy. Large chunks of everyday reality seemed to retreat into a fog. Still, despite the deepening gloom brought on by his ailments and the gradual waning of his physical powers, his innate will to live and wry humor kept asserting themselves. A smile of painful wisdom could at any moment transfigure the despondency of his old age. Once so impatient, he settled quite gracefully for a life that not only moved at a snail's pace, but required frequent stopovers to rest the snail. In 1949 he wrote a friend that he was like an old car that already had 100,000 miles on its back, but could not forget the horsepower it had commanded in its prime. Fully aware that such nostalgia was unwise, he took comfort in the thought that only fools expect wisdom of themselves and others.

His daily routine was increasingly dictated to him by Dr. Jakob Stahel, who in the late forties was Jung's physician. But Jung would also sometimes ask for advice and accept treatment from other physicians, especially if, like his follower Ignaz Tauber, they were less strict than old Dr. Stahel with regard to such pleasures as smoking. For in spite of his series of embolisms, Jung adamantly refused to give up his cherished habit of smoking. He pleaded, almost pathetically, for permission to smoke three pipesful of tobacco a day, plus one or two "miniature cigars." A little bit of tobacco, he argued, helped him concentrate. Like Freud, he defied time and again doctors' orders in this matter. Jung being Jung, it took a premonitory dream to make him finally give up smoking. The sacrifice put him in a terrible mood at first. "What do the gods expect without the soothing incense?" he wailed, and held onto the extinguished pipe, carrying it around like some ritual object, fondling it or sucking in cold, tobacco-scented air with his declining lung power.

Hardly less annoying to him was the strict regime he was made to follow in his daily life. His working time was greatly abridged and often did not extend beyond two or three hours in the morning. Long periods of rest were prescribed and lengthy walks, which Jung undertook in every kind of weather. His social life was also curtailed—visits to the Psychological Club became rare, and he received fewer callers at home.

No medical edicts could keep him, however, from an event that was a high point in his social life: Winston Churchill's visit to Zurich in the fall of 1946. The University of Zurich marked the occasion with a formal dinner at which Jung was seated next to Churchill. Afterwards, Jung kept alluding proudly to this solemn affair. He wrote a friend that he had "nearly collapsed with surprise" upon discovering that his was the seat of honor beside Churchill. This had restored his faith in "signs and miracles." He also intimated that conversation with Churchill had been difficult, in that the Englishman seemed to direct most of his answers to Jung's questions to the House of Commons. Yet when Churchill, visibly tired, assured him in parting that the Zurich reception had been the most moving of his lifetime, Jung was eager to believe even that tarnished bit of politeness.

Most frustrating about this phase of Jung's life for him was that, as his capacity for work was declining, he was seized by a new burst of creativity. His brain teemed with unformed ideas. He found it next to impossible to keep pace with his fertile unconscious. He felt, he said jokingly, as if he were the ancestral mother of the whole rabbit family. In the midst of this creative ferment, his labors as therapist became increasingly irksome to him. Forced to husband his waning psychic resources, he began to experience therapeutic work as an unbearable drain. Where once the practice of analysis and his creative work had complemented each other, now the two were in open conflict. He even attributed some of his physical ailments to his neglect of his creative impulses: his shortchanged creativity simply avenged itself—so he imagined—on his vulnerable body. Hence he decided that he must drop almost all his analytic work. To friends who came to see him he said outright that he could no longer plumb the depths of their psyches; with the inevitable egotism of old age, he was going to save his remaining energy for his own purposes.

There was one form of energy expenditure, however, that Jung absolutely refused to curtail: his correspondence. The Allied victory over Hitler freed Switzerland from the isolation of the war years, and Jung was suddenly deluged by letters. Even though he moaned at the flood of mail assailing him, he answered it not only conscientiously but often at great length and with obvious gusto. He enjoyed letter writing because it is a fairly nonobtrusive form of human interaction; it shields a sensitive introvert like Jung from too direct contact with others while offering him great latitude of expression. The letter writer who is an introvert can avoid the banalities of small talk without being cramped by the self-consciousness that usually goes with writing for publication. Hence one finds in many of Jung's letters a freshness and immediacy one seeks in vain in the books he composed with posterity in mind. He dealt with all sorts of things in his correspondence, from the most mundane to ultimate metaphysical questions. For instance, an American wrote to ask if he had ever seen a woman who was entirely helpless. Yes, Jung replied, but only when there was a man nearby. Queries from every corner of the globe, from friend and stranger alike, were all handled with the same meticulous care. Jung refused to take easy outs, believing as he did that every question put to him in writing deserved a thoughtful reply.[1] The barrage of mail from all over not only made demands on Jung but also indicated that his fame was spreading over an ever widening area. This knowledge soothed his pride that had been wounded by the indifference and mockery of people in his own country.

The class of correspondents Jung preferred was made up of Protestant and Catholic clergymen. With them he could discuss, ad infinitum, the matters of religion and theology that had held him spellbound since adolescence. It often appears in those letters as though the apostate psychiatrist were carrying on a posthumous dialogue with his father, martyred by secret doubt, and with his theologian uncles. He seems hardly to have noticed that many of these simple pastors were not of a stature to keep up with his flights of thought. The urge to confess and justify himself was simply so overwhelming as to blind him to the inadequacies of his confessors.

The ranks of letter writers also included people who were to

[1]Occasionally, though, when he felt provoked, Jung could be very abrasive in his letters.

become close friends of the aging and despondent psychiatrist. Among them was the British Dominican Victor White, a classical scholar thoroughly familiar with Jung's work. In an early letter to White, Jung paid him the heavy-handed compliment of saying that his understanding of Jungian psychology made him a "queer bird" among theologians.[2] There ensued a lively exchange of letters running often to many pages. In a short time, the two men met and became friends. A warmth unusual for Jung developed, but was soon dispelled by Jung's prickliness. Once again he was haunted by the feeling that everybody misread him. He prized this autumn friendship but could do little to prevent its collapse. Even when he was apparently discussing a metaphysical problem, like the meaning of evil, an undercurrent of personal pique would creep into his letters of that period. At first, he had written most of them in longhand; by and by, he had his secretary type them from dictation. He would return to longhand whenever the friendship flared up again, then revert once more, disillusioned, to the machine. Manuscript and typescript were the barometers of a friendship that began in great hope, then cooled markedly, without dying altogether.

Another of Jung's late friendships that began through letters was to prove more resilient. This friendship was, in fact, a double one, involving the Winterthur physician Ignaz Tauber and his wife Elsbeth. If Victor White's knowledge of Jungian psychology made him a rare bird among theologians, Ignaz

---

[2]Like Churchill, Jung could be most generous with polite compliments. His letters are filled with assurances that the present correspondent is the only person understanding him and that this comes as a great relief to a man so monumentally misunderstood. For those correspondents who lived long enough to see Jung's letters published, it must have come as a surprise to discover how many of these "only persons" existed within Jung's sphere.

Tauber was equally singular among Swiss general practitioners. It would never have occurred to them to treat bone fractures, influenza, or the common cold with the aid of Jungian psychology. True, it was all the rage at the time to speak of the "psychosomatic" origins of many illnesses, but in practice doctors relied on aspirin, plaster casts, and the up-and-coming antibiotics. Not so Ignaz Tauber. Admittedly, he needed repeated urging before he deigned to examine the work on Jungian psychology his book dealer sent him. He returned the volume three times, in fact, before his resistance wore down. But then he became totally captivated. Elsbeth's reaction was stronger still, bordering on the ecstatic. Early in 1946, the couple wrote a joint letter to Jung expressing their admiration. They enclosed a very Jungian-sounding poem composed by Ignaz. Jung's reply, though delayed, was uncommonly warm. He explained that he was almost drowning in correspondence. But since the male part of the couple was a poet, he could assuredly concoct as many answers from Jung as he liked, and thus bring a soft glow into the eyes of the feminine half. Actually, a royal pair like them did not really depend on letters from others for, according to an old saying, they could find everything they needed within themselves. Somewhat later he invited the Taubers to Küsnacht and found them to his liking. Elsbeth and Ignaz decided to undergo Jungian analysis. Jung who was then withdrawing from analytic work passed the couple on to two of his students. He did agree, though, to keep an eye on their progress and to discuss sticky points with them on occasion.

With the zeal of the new convert, Ignaz Tauber began to use Jungian notions in his medical practice. Along with pills and injections, he treated his patients to large doses of analytic psychology. In the process, he tended to fall into a preachy tone, so that many a bedridden patient who had greeted his arrival with the usual "God bless you, doctor" came to grace his departure with an inadvertent "Goodbye, Reverend!" Far from being put out by the confusion of roles, Tauber actually grew to enjoy it.

Jung visited the Tauber home in Winterthur repeatedly, chatting amiably with the children and generally having a good time. He was highly amused whenever the baby of the family, little Marianne, would wipe off his paternal kiss with the back of her hand. And when Ignaz related a dream in which he, Ignaz, had played an unflattering part, Jung felt free to laugh uproariously. The subject of the dream was a get-together of the Taubers and the Jungs. In front of each of the four was a plate with a peach. But while the peaches of the others were gloriously ripe, the one in front of Ignaz was still unripe, yet rotten already. When Jung had recovered from his amusement, he merely advised that, as long as Tauber's dream fruits rotted prematurely, he would be unlikely to bring the literary efforts he was then engaged in to fruition.

What made Jung's dealings with Ignaz Tauber so different from his other friendships with men was the fact that Tauber was not undone by Jung's occasional acerbity. Jung once boasted to Tauber that he himself was able to accept criticism that would drive others crazy. Be that as it may, some time later Tauber was to remember this remark when Jung mercilessly panned some writing he had done on Egyptian mythology. Although many people would have reacted with hurt, Tauber knew Jung's harsh criticism to be justified. His loyalty did not go unrewarded; time and again Jung consulted him in matters touching on his health. Jung was grateful also that Tauber kept his distance from the intrigues of the Psychological Club; grateful enough, in fact, to present Ignaz with some tokens of his favor, including a friendship ring of debatable esthetic value.

Another relationship that became increasingly important to the aging Jung was that to his female disciple Jolan Jacobi, whose first name evolved during the process of individuation to Jolande. A Jewish convert to Catholicism, she was the daughter of a Hungarian industrialist who was to commit suicide to escape capture by the Gestapo. Jung met her first in the late twenties when, as vice-president of the Cultural League of Vienna, she repeatedly invited him to lecture in the Austrian capital. Even then Jung was impressed by her seemingly inexhaustible energy.

With her frenetic zeal she promoted the initially quite vague plans of publisher Daniel Brody to issue an international journal with Jung as editor. The goal of this enterprise was nothing less than a synthesis of the most diverse sciences, from theology to astrophysics. While Jung was intrigued by the project, it also weighed heavily upon him. He repeatedly apprised Jolan Jacobi of his fear that the whole idea was premature. Besides, he argued, his name, which would be on the masthead, was not yet familiar enough in the German-speaking world to attract readers.

But the faint-heartedness of her champion could not discourage Jolan Jacobi. She pursued the realization of the project with such spirit that Jung offered her a post as editor. He compared her to Saint Catherine of Alexandria, the early Christian martyr who, legend has it, converted the Christian-hating wife of Emperor Maxentius, and many of his courtiers, to her faith. "For the imponderables of this world and its window-dressing," Jung wrote her, "the Church Fathers, as we know, always need a shrewd Catherine d'Alexandrie."

All this admiration notwithstanding, Jung did not exactly despair when the project collapsed, for it had made excessive demands on his time and energy. As it often is with establishing a journal, the enterprise had gone no further than the tentative selection of a name—Jung suggested *Weltanschauung*—the compilation of an inflated list of potential contributors, and some jockeying for the post of managing editor (Jung was to act as editor-in-chief). A preliminary meeting of some of the principals apparently confirmed Jung's suspicion that, all of the publisher's assurances to the contrary, the bulk of the editorial work would be borne by him. When this arrangement proved unacceptable to Jung, the whole project aborted. He explained to Jolande Jacobi that the proud falcon her energy had helped to send aloft had returned home, utterly disheveled, to crawl back into its shell. But he felt no personal regret, he said, since he already had more than enough work without this new project (whose collapse came in April of 1933, shortly before he was to assume leadership of the newly Nazified *Zentralblatt fuer Psychotherapie und ihre Grenzgebiete*).

The failure did not prevent Jolande Jacobi from setting herself up as Jung's public relations manager for Austria. She employed every available means to win a wider public for his ideas. Jung had to tone down her zeal at times, declining a number of her lecture invitations with the excuse of too much other work. But he was amenable to the task of analyzing her dreams by mail.

As long as Jolande Jacobi remained in Vienna, at a safe distance from him, Jung willingly countenanced most of the missionary work of this energetic disciple. But in 1938, fleeing from the Nazis, Mrs. Jacobi moved to Zurich, where she rededicated her life to the practice and propagation of Jungian psychology. So close at hand, the militance of his devotee was distressing to Jung. Obtrusiveness was a byproduct of Jolande Jacobi's fierce energy, and tact was not her strong point. Over a period of time, her enthusiasm could become wearing, and Jung had to employ doses of sarcasm in order to keep her at arm's length. In his appraisals of her analytic method, Jung would repeatedly point out her tendency to take too active a part, to interpret instead of letting things speak for themselves. He warned her not to become entangled in the witches' sabbath of her patients' neuroses, indicating that this was neither wise nor therapeutically fruitful. He also admonished her to guard her tongue, which inclined to be sharp and unprofessional.

Jung's association with his students was much like that of any other founder of a new school or sect. His admiring disciples were not only his support, but also a cross he had to bear; they not only disseminated his ideas, but distorted them in the process. Not content to act as his mouthpiece, they used the mantle of his authority to smuggle their own shallow ideas into the public arena. But the prophet of a new religion does not really choose his apostles; nor can he really control them. Whatever misgivings Jung may have had on this score, he simply could not stop Jolande Jacobi from becoming the chief interpreter of Jungian psychology. As such she was cited, more and more, by Jungians, non-Jungians, and anti-Jungians alike.

Given her enterprising nature, she was bound to hit upon the idea of founding an institute for Jungian psychology.[3] She

---

[3]As early as 1939, in fact, she had suggested to Jung that they set up an institute, but the war put a temporary end to the plan.

pushed this project with the fierce determination she had shown earlier in the matter of a Jungian journal. By 1947, the project had begun to take shape. This time she had resolved not to be sidetracked by any doubts or pusillanimity, not even from Jung himself, who actually was rather dubious about the notion of institutionalizing his psychology. He had often stressed that he was neither a prophet nor the founder of a new sect, that he was not a "Jungian" himself, and that his was not a proselytizing temperament. Yet he always made these disclaimers in a tone of voice that left room to doubt their finality. Hence Jolande Jacobi would not be swayed by Jung's misgivings. Jung finally realized that this woman was an elemental force it would be senseless to resist. It had cost him great effort earlier to divert her from another pet project: the founding of a *Catholic* institute of Jungian psychology. This time he would yield to the inevitable.

There was some bickering over the naming of the new institute. Jung thought it should not carry his name, but something less personal, like "Institute for Complex Psychology." He would have a hard time, he said, getting used to the idea that C. G. Jung referred not only to a private person but to a thing as well. Yet in the end he yielded, once again, to Jolande Jacobi and her party. The "C. G. Jung Institute" was christened in April 1948. It was hardly majestic, occupying a few modest chambers on the second floor of the Psychological Club's quarters on Gemeindestrasse. The Club took the fledgling institute under its wing, endowing it with a christening gift of 100,000 Swiss francs. Its first curators, aside from Jung and Jacobi, were C. A. Meier, Liliane Frey, and Kurt Binswanger; its first secretary was Aniela Jaffé. And from 1948 until 1960, Jolande Jacobi was charged with overseeing the curriculum.

In his inaugural speech Jung outlined some of the goals of the institute. It was to conduct research on dreams and symbol analysis, mythology, and the psychology of religion, but also in the area of experimental psychology. The institute was not to realize Jung's vision of pioneering research; over the years, it assumed the shape of a training center for Jungian analysts. In preparing for the diploma, candidates were required to undergo a Jungian analysis of 300 hours, in addition to the theoretical course of study.

It is noteworthy that every one of the thirteen full-time members of the institute's first class, anno 1948, was either British or American. From the start most lectures and seminars were held in English—a custom that still holds today. Even the signs on the doors were in English, or bilingual. In the sixties, when the count of regular students swelled to about 150, British and Americans continued to form the main contingent of a student body drawn from many nations. By the seventies, students started to arrive from Catholic countries (Italy, France) heretofore impervious to Jungian psychology.

Jung viewed the institute that bore his name with a mixture of satisfaction and grave doubts. He had no illusions about the mediocrity of most of the faculty. The dearth of original research disappointed him. Recognizing the dangers that attended the institutionalizing of his psychology, he warned against a stance of infallibilism, against embalming the body of his work and treating it as holy writ. The institute was too tiny and vulnerable, he felt, to provoke the powers-that-be with brazen dogmatism. He also foresaw that the institute might, under the sway of self-willed apostles, move far afield from the original impulses of his psychology.

Carl Jung did not gain in his lifetime the universal recognition he yearned for. He had to rest content with the status of cult hero. His hope was that the new Aquarian age whose dawn he was one of the first to herald would enshrine him after his death as a major prophet. The founding of the Jung Institute, when he was almost seventy-three, stands as a crucial step in the process of his transfiguration. In the thirteen years remaining to him, the reality of his person receded further and further into the aura of the wise old seer of Lake Zurich, further and further behind the Institute that was to become the mystical body of Carl Gustav Jung.

EPILOGUE

The last major work of Jung bears the title *Mysterium Conjunctionis*. "Conjunction" is an alchemical term for the union of the opposites that "confront one another in enmity or attract each other in love." Jung, as was his wont, psychologized the term, and used it to refer to the process of psychic integration giving birth to the "higher ego," the self.

The quest for the great synthesis that would still the yearning of the halves to become whole was the leitmotiv, not only of Jung's work, but also of his life. From the moment he first became aware of his inner split, Jung felt compelled to search for the magic nostrum that would cure his psychic wound. Viewing his inner rent as expressive less of a personal condition than of a basic disorder of the universe, Jung was haunted by the thought of "the dreadful double aspect" of God in whom "a sea of grace is met by a seething lake of fire." From the touchy irritability with which Yahweh treated his Chosen People, Jung concluded that the Almighty Himself was afflicted with dissociation. Jung's great cure would have to encompass not only suffering mankind, but God Himself.

Thus God became involved rather early, and on many levels, in Jung's attempts to heal the lacerating split within his own psyche. Reading his father's existential shipwreck as the tragedy of the dutiful man of God "with whom faith broke faith," Jung soon came to equate neurotic and spiritual suffering, and he never veered from this facile equation. In this way the struggle for mental health became a search for salvation; psychotherapy, a "cure of souls"; the plumbing of the unconscious, a confrontation with God.

In Jung's curious amalgamation of religious concerns with the imperatives of mental hygiene, *symbol* and *myth* were designated as the crucial conduits, the areas of contact between the material and the spiritual. In Jung's view, it was man's estrangement from the mythical realm, and the subsequent shrinking of his existence to the merely factual, that was the major cause of mental illness. If this be so, then perhaps the apparently most senseless gestures of those we call insane can be invested with the dignity of meaning by their insertion into a larger mythical context. Inversely, Jung said, strip a figure of supreme religious potency, such as Jesus Christ, of his transcendent aura, and his most sublime utterances are apt to crumble into the rubble of amorphous nonsense. Without this mythical sanction, statements like "I am the way, and the truth, and the life, and no one comes to the Father but by me" decay into the gibberish of a rabbi who is not quite right in the head. It is the function of religion, Jung said, "to link us back to the eternal myth."

But in Jung's time, the Christian myth had collapsed, as evidenced—or so Jung thought—by the tragedy of his father. Jung originally tried to put Christians (or Jews) who had lost their faith back in touch with their traditional religion, but to little avail. The loss of vitality, and of healing power, by the Christian religion meant that the God of Western man had emigrated from His Church. Jung's vision in early puberty of God dropping a gigantic piece of turd on His cathedral was a drastic image of the true state of affairs. But if God had gone into hiding—and Jung did not believe for a moment that He had died—where was He to be found? Jung discovered Him literally underground, in the subterranean caves of his dream images, in the catacombs of the psyche known as the region of the unconscious. A cataclysmic spiritual shift had taken place, largely missed by the theologians, a shift from the God above to the God below, from communal liturgy to private communion, from ritual observance to emotional experience, from dogma to myth, from religion to psychology, from the conscious to the unconscious.

The unconscious became the main focus and point of reference of Jung's spiritual science. As refuge of the Divine, as abode of symbol and myth, the Jungian unconscious was raised far above the humble station of the Freudian id from which it derived. A brief comparison of Freud's and Jung's notions of the unconscious may prove instructive. Whereas Freud imagined the unconscious as a chaos of seething libidinal energies, Jung viewed it as a *cosmos*, with an intrinsic order and creativity of its own. While Freud saw the unconscious as a crude storage area for undigested personal traumata, Jung conceived of it as the rich and vast treasure chamber of the archetypes. When both men use the same ocean-land metaphor to illustrate the relationship between the unconscious and consciousness, the differences of their conceptions are highlighted. Freud took it for granted that consciousness had a greater personal and cultural value than the unconscious. Defining psychoanalysis as an effort to expand the rule of the ego at the expense of the id, he likened analytic work to the arduous reclaiming of arable land from the sea. While Freud thus stressed the intractability and barrenness of the "ocean" of the unconscious, Jung was struck by its immense wealth of living creatures, its "bounty beyond our fathoming." In its infinite vastness, Jung felt, the unconscious defies any attempt to plumb its depth, to catalogue its abundance, to bridle its elemental dynamism. The ocean cannot be drained, and it is futile presumption on the ego's part to want to annex segments of the unconscious. In Jung's canon, the only appropriate attitude of consciousness vis-à-vis the unconscious is reverence. Only if consciousness, recognizing its relative puniness, pays heed to the injunctions issuing from the unconscious, can it play its role as the light that comprehends the darkness.

For Jung the interplay between consciousness and the unconscious was yet another form of the cosmic duality, of the warring peace, that haunted him. The two psychic opposites are commutual, in that unconsciousness without consciousness is blind, and consciousness without the unconscious is impotent. Their strife must be overcome by the "higher copulation" that gives birth to the unity of the self. The most poignant expression of Jung's lifelong struggle to achieve this great synthesis was his *Answer to Job.*

Job was one of those fated books Jung felt *compelled* to write, almost in spite of himself. He came by it, he said, "the way a dog comes by a thrashing." The result of this thrashing from on high was a many-layered tract. It represented Jung's settling of accounts with the liberal clergy's sanitized God, all-loving, of infinite mercy—and unbearably insipid to a man of Jung's temper. It chronicled Jung's most direct confrontation with the ruthless, wanton, demonic side of God with which Job (and Jung) had collided in such a traumatic manner. And it constituted Jung's ultimate attempt to cancel the distance between the Divine and himself.

By trifling captiously with Job's devotion, and by silencing Job's demand for justice with a bullying display of raw power, the Biblical Yahweh had exhibited a sovereign disregard for the moral law he had promulgated among men. But in grinding Job into the dust, merely because of Satan's dare, Yahweh had suffered a moral defeat at the hands of his creature. More importantly, Job had given indications of possessing a greater degree of consciousness than Yahweh; he appeared to have recognized the dissociation of Yahweh's nature of which Yahweh Himself was unaware.

It was originally man's puniness and frailty, Jung held, that led him to develop "a somewhat keener consciousness based on self-reflection." Yahweh in his omnipotence could afford to remain unconscious. After the Job episode, however, Yahweh came gradually to suspect that His creature might have outstripped Him in the matter of self-awareness. According to Jung, Yahweh's realization of this amazing, and scandalous, state of affairs gave rise to His desire to regenerate Himself. Thus the process of God's incarnation in the *Son of Man* was set in motion. In other words, Yahweh's autocratic excesses vis-à-vis Job, and His discovery of Job's superior consciousness, led directly to His resolve to bring about a rapprochement with man by His becoming flesh in Jesus Christ.

But God's incarnation in Christ was merely a first step. It was to be followed, sooner or later, by the *Christification of many*, by God entering into empirical man. God's continuing embrace of His creature was eventually going to produce a new race of God-men. Had not Christ himself with his "You are gods" foretold this triumphant apotheosis of man?

God's embodiment in man, Jung thought, was really the same as the process of individuation. God was just another name for the archetype of the self, expressive of the same psychic reality. To distinguish between the two, and to split hairs about their ontological difference, would only distance man from God and might even "prevent God from becoming man."

The myth of the emergence of the God-man was the culmination of Jung's quest for the great synthesis that would resolve his inner duality. This quest also led Jung to propound a variety of other syntheses: the fusion of religion and empiricism in analytic psychology; the coupling of ego and unconscious in the archetype of the self; the confluence of spirit and matter in the symbols of alchemy; the blending of the singular and the universal in the collective unconscious.

But in the last analysis Jung's search for the Holy Grail of conjunction failed. His syntheses did not eventuate in genuine union; they were makeshift soldering jobs, contrived amalgamations, rather than transcendent integrations of the opposites.

In the intellectual realm, Jung's great synthesis remained very much at the level of mere verbal operations whose superficialities were concealed by an impressive array of erudition. Jung's often-noted lack of lucidity, his turgid style, the leakiness of his logic, his inability to distinguish between hypotheses and facts are as many telltale signs of this lack of integration. And the biographical events we have chronicled at some length reflect the same failure in the existential realm.

If Carl Jung's figure is nevertheless of more than passing interest it is not only because his individual patienthood anticipated a collective one. It is true that his evangelism was defeated in the end by the cautious conservatism and the concern for his own safety that may be commendable social traits but are not usually counted among the credentials of great prophets. But Jung did have an acute sensitivity for the dilemmas increasingly bedeviling our culture. And if his psychology is murky, its vindication of the subjective realm, of the psychic kingdom within, has advanced the cultural process of the redefinition of reality that in settled periods of history is mainly the business of artists and philosophers, but that in the present dark times crucially involves those philosophers in spite of themselves—psychologists and madmen.

BIBLIOGRAPHY

ADLER, G. *Studies in Analytical Psychology.* New York: G. P. Putnam's Sons, 1969.

BALLY, G. *Deutschstämmige Psychotherapie?* Neue Zürcher Zeitung, CLV, no. 343 (1934).

BENNET, E. A. *C. G. Jung.* New York: Dutton, 1961.

———. *What Jung Really Said.* London: Macdonald, 1966.

BLOCH, E. *Das Prinzip Hoffnung.* Frankfurt: Suhrkamp, 1959.

BOSS, M. Untitled chapter in Pongratz, L. J., *Psychotherapie in Selbstdarstellungen.* Bern: Hans Huber, 1973.

BURCKHARDT, C. J. and Rychner, M. *Briefe: 1926–1965,* edited by Claudia Mertz-Rychner. Frankfurt: Fischer, 1970.

ELLENBERGER, H. F. *The Discovery of the Unconscious.* New York: Basic Books, 1970.

ERIKSON, E. H. *Young Man Luther.* New York: Norton, 1958.

259

C. G. Jung—The Haunted Prophet

EVANS, R. I. *Conversations with Carl Jung and Reactions from Ernest Jones.* New York: Van Nostrand, 1964.

FIERZ, H. K. *Klinik und Analytische Psychologie.* Zurich: Rascher, 1963.

FORDHAM, F. *An Introduction to Jung's Psychology.* Baltimore: Penguin Books, 1953.

FORDHAM, M., ed. *Contact with Jung.* London: Tavistock Publications, 1963.

FOREL, A. *Briefe: 1864–1927,* edited by H. H. Walser. Bern: Hans Huber, 1968.

FREUD, S. *Letters of Sigmund Freud,* edited by E. L. Freud. New York: Basic Books, 1960.

———. "The History of the Psychoanalytic Movement." *Psychoanalytic Review,* 3, 406–454. (Transl: A. A. Brill.)

FREUD, S. and JUNG, C. G. *The Freud/Jung Letters,* edited by W. McGuire. Princeton: Princeton University Press, 1974.

FREUD, S. and PFISTER, O. *Briefe: 1909–1939,* edited by E. L. Freud and H. Meng. Frankfurt: Fischer, 1963.

HÄBERLIN, P. *Statt einer Autobiographie.* Frauenfeld: Huber, 1959.

HOSTIE, R. *Religion and the Psychology of Jung.* London: Sheed and Ward, 1957.

JACOBI, J. *Psychology of C. G. Jung* (revised edition). New Haven: Yale Univ. Press, 1963.

JAFFÉ, A. *From the Life and Work of C. G. Jung.* New York: Harper and Row, 1971.

JAMES, W. *Pragmatism.* New York: Longmans, Green and Co., 1907.

JASPERS, K. *Allgemeine Psychopathologie* (6th edition). Berlin: Springer, 1953.

JONES, E. *The Life and Work of Sigmund Freud* (3 vols.). New York: Basic Books, 1953.

Jung, C. G. *Briefe* (3 vols.). Olten: Walter, 1972.

————. *The Collected Works* (17 vols.), edited by G. Adler et al. Princeton: Princeton Univ. Press, 1954–1971.

————. *Letters* (Vol. I), edited by G. Adler and A. Jaffe. Princeton: Princeton Univ. Press, 1973.

————. *Man and His Symbols.* New York: Doubleday, 1969.

————. *Memories, Dreams, Reflections.* New York: Pantheon Books, 1963.

Jung, E. *Animus und Anima.* Zurich: Rascher, 1967.

Keyserling, H. *Das Reisetagebuch eines Philosophen.* Darmstadt: Rolle, 1956.

————. *Reise durch die Zeit* (Part III). Innsbruck: Verlag der Palme, 1963.

Kretschmer, E. *Gestalten und Gedanken.* Stuttgart: Thieme, 1963.

Mann, T. *Three Essays.* New York: Knopf, 1929.

Marcuse, L. *Mein Zwanzigstes Jahrhundert.* Frankfurt: Fischer, 1968.

Oeri, A. "Ein paar Jungenderrinnerungen," in *Die kulterelle Bedeutung der komplexen Psychologie.* Berlin: Springer, 1935.

Progoff, I. *Jung, Synchronicity, and Human Destiny.* New York: Julian Press, 1973.

————. *Jung's Psychology and Its Social Meaning.* New York: Julian Press, 1953.

Rexroth, K. *With Eye and Ear.* New York: Herder and Herder, 1970.

Rieff, P. *The Triumph of the Therapeutic.* New York: Harper and Row, 1966.

Rychner, M. and Burckhardt, C. J. *Briefe: 1926–1965,* edited by Claudia Mertz-Rychner. Frankfurt: Fischer, 1970.

SAPIR, E. *Selected Writings.* Berkeley: Univ. of California Press, 1958.

SERRANO, M. *C. G. Jung and Hermann Hesse, A Record of Two Friendships.* New York: Schocken Books, 1966.

STORR, A. *C. G. Jung.* New York: Viking Press, 1973.

WALSER, H. H. *Das Schicksal des Psychoanalytikers Johann Jakob Honegger 1885–1911.* New York: Spring Publications, 1974.

WEHR, G. *Portrait of Jung.* New York: Herder and Herder, 1971.

WHITE, V. *God and the Unconscious.* London: Harvill Press, 1952.

WOLFF, T. *Studien zu C. G. Jungs Psychologie.* Zurich: Rhein-Verlag, 1959.

INDEX

Numbers in italics refer to entries in Bibliography.

Index

7 53 -1776

Isa the Young

4725
32
1950
1425
___
17700